TRANSNATIONAL
TERROR

AEI-Hoover
policy studies

The studies in this series are issued jointly
by the American Enterprise Institute
for Public Policy Research and the Hoover
Institution on War, Revolution and Peace.
They are designed to focus on
policy problems of current and future interest,
to set forth the factors underlying
these problems and to evaluate
courses of action available to policymakers.
The views expressed in these studies
are those of the authors and do not necessarily
reflect the views of the staff, officers
or members of the governing boards of
AEI or the Hoover Institution.

TRANSNATIONAL TERROR

J. Bowyer Bell

American Enterprise Institute for Public Policy Research
Washington, D. C.

Hoover Institution on War, Revolution and Peace
Stanford University, Stanford, California

AEI-Hoover Policy Study 17, September 1975
(Hoover Institution Studies 53)

Third printing, July 1979
Second printing, January 1978
ISBN 0-8447-3187-0

Library of Congress Catalog Card No. 75-27369

Printed in the United States of America

Contents

Preface

This study arises from my long-standing interest in revolutionary violence, an interest that has regularly taken me on extensive tours to interview those involved. It is based on thousands of interview hours and endless conversations on strategy and tactics with the revolutionaries and their opponents. Few of these rebels would consider themselves terrorists, and few would probably agree with my conclusions. Be that as it may, any study of terrorist activities must be largely qualitative and, since conventional academic approaches do not work in this field, dependent on less than rigorous sources. This is particularly true of the section on Latin America, in which only a general overview and concentration on a few cases is possible. Being bombed in Belfast, arrested in the Middle East, and expelled in Africa are not really very academic activities in any case.

I should like to thank Ted Gurr, Irving L. Horowitz, Ted Ropp, and others brought together in Virginia by Trevor Dupuy; also Ambassador Lewis Hoffacker and his staff at the State Department; Robert McBrien at Treasury; T. W. Adams for aid and comfort in Washington; the members of the Survey Discussion Group on International Terrorism of the Council on Foreign Relations in New York; the international terror panel at the International Studies Association chaired by Carol Baumann; and Harold Lasswell and William T. R. Fox for letting me try out a few ideas in their world politics seminar.

J. Bowyer Bell
August 1975

1

An Analysis of Terror

What matter the victims provided
the gesture is beautiful?

Laurent Tailhade

Terror: Historical and Definitional Problems

On 17 December 1973, five young men—tall, with olive complexions
and moustaches—arrived from Madrid at Rome's Leonardo da Vinci
International Airport and made their way to the transit lounge. Shortly
before 1:00 P.M., the five appeared in a group of passengers moving
toward a metal-detector booth and search area. Beyond this last security
barrier the embarkation gate led to three parked jetliners, including a
Pan American 707 and a Lufthansa 737. At the moment the five men—
Palestinian guerrillas—reached the barrier, they pulled submachine guns
from their hand luggage and lunged forward firing into the crowd at
the gate. The plate glass walls of the terminal building shattered;
passengers and airport personnel ran for cover or fell to the floor. As
three of the guerrillas rounded up the Italian security men—killing one
with a burst of machine-gun fire when he attempted to escape—the
other two guerrillas tossed incendiary grenades into the Pan Am 707.
The passengers aboard were trapped in the swirling smoke and spreading
fire. As the crew struggled to get the passengers out, the two guerrillas
rushed back to join their colleagues who had taken over the Lufthansa
737. The pilot was ordered to take off. By this time the toll on the
ground had reached thirty-one dead, mostly aboard the Pan Am aircraft.

Once in the air, the guerrillas demanded to be flown to Beirut.
Beirut authorities refused to allow the plane to land—an increasingly
favored response of involuntary host airports to skyjackers. Landing
finally at Athens, the Palestinians found the airport ringed with military
units and security police. Threatening to blow up the plane, the guerrillas

demanded the release of two Arabs, Black September guerrillas who had been arrested in August 1973 after shooting up the transit lounge of the Athens airport, killing three people and wounding fifty. When the Greek authorities delayed, the captain of the Lufthansa aircraft reported by radio that the guerrillas had already killed four hostages and threatened to continue killing more until the Greeks released the Black Septembrists. Although later it was learned that the guerrillas had actually killed only one hostage, bringing the total death toll to thirty-two, the Greek authorities announced that they would release the two guerrillas. When neither of the released prisoners could be persuaded to board the skyjacked aircraft, the jet took off without them, beginning a search for an airport that would accept the guerrillas and their hostages. Finding no takers, the captain was forced to land in Kuwait without permission or assistance from the airport control tower. The Kuwaiti authorities reluctantly accepted the parcel.[1] The five guerrillas were imprisoned, the hostages released, and one more spectacular terrorist drama in the name of Palestine came to an end.

The episode aroused almost universal condemnation. In Beirut, *An Nahar,* Lebanon's leading newspaper, felt that the killings had placed "a burden on the Arab conscience at a moment when the plight of the Palestinian people was starting to be a burden on the conscience of the world."[2] Pope Paul VI denounced the act as senseless, "offensive to both human and Christian dignity."[3] Coming on the eve of the Geneva talks arranged by American Secretary of State Henry Kissinger—talks which promised some hope of a Middle East accommodation that would take into account the aspirations of the Palestinians—the massacre appeared a mad and futile act. A statement (signed, "The Palestine People") which appeared in Beirut, announcing that the operation had been aimed at Americans because of the airlift of weapons to Israel during the October War, appeased no one—in part because four of the victims had been Moroccan officials. The Palestine Liberation Organization (PLO) refused to accept this rationale and condemned the attack as having worked against Palestinian interests.

---

[1] The Kuwaiti authorities had earlier been faced with a similar situation with another skyjacked jet landing without permission. The Kuwaiti solution to that had been to send the five Arab guerrillas to the Syrian front during the 1973 October War, where all were killed in action—a statistical oddity that might have given less desperate men pause.

[2] *New York Times,* 18 December 1973.

[3] Ibid.

Kuwait began arrangements to send the five guerrillas to the PLO to be tried by their own people, but this was insufficient for many who felt that the international community could not and should not tolerate further terrorist assaults. As the *New York Times* remarked editorially:

> The indiscriminate murder of 32 innocent persons by five Arab hijackers at the Rome and Athens airports is a crime that must not be allowed to go unpunished. . . .
>
> This latest crime against humanity does not even have the political excuse sometimes advanced in defense of terrorism. To shoot up innocent bystanders in any airport lounge, to toss incendiary bombs into a passenger plane, then to hijack another plane and murder an innocent "hostage" in cold blood is savage barbarism. . . .
>
> The Government of Kuwait has an obligation before mankind to see that justice is done. Whether it tries the terrorists itself or cooperates with Italy's extradition request, it must move to put them before a duly constituted court. To release them or to turn them over to the guerrilla Palestine Liberation—even if the P.L.O. proposed to undertake punishment—would be a travesty of governmental responsibility.[4]

This *Times* editorial reflects the usual Western response to political terrorism: outraged moral indignation coupled with a demand for swift justice by sanctioned means. There could be no political "excuse" for the murder of innocents, only prompt and appropriate punishment.

Not all observers were able to judge so unequivocally, although many found it hard to accept the Black September argument that anyone traveling to Israel, no matter what his nationality, is an enemy of Palestine and that anyone aboard an American airliner could be a legitimate Palestinian target. Still, some drew swift parallels to the death of innocents at American hands in Hiroshima and Nagasaki. Others asked if the more recent use of American B-52s over Hanoi was an appropriate military exercise, while the Palestinian use of incendiary grenades in Rome was not. And, it was asked, given Palestinian objectives, could the Rome incident really be called senseless when those meeting in Geneva would do so under a Palestinian shadow? Proponents of this view argued that to brand the Rome massacre a "crime against humanity" would be the first step by the comfortable and powerful towards limiting the weapons available to those rebels everywhere who wage unconventional war for the weak against institutionalized injustice or repressive regimes.

---

[4] *New York Times*, 28 December 1973.

The United Nations General Assembly's refusal to take action on an anti-terrorist resolution only a few months before the events in Rome and Athens revealed the division of world opinion over the question of terrorism. In fact, those proceedings could not even produce a satisfactory definition of terror, even though few ever have difficulty recognizing the deed itself. In the face of an ever escalating cycle of spectacular terror dramas, there is remarkably little understanding of the terrorist phenomenon or of the means to fashion an appropriate and effective response.

History and Terror. International order has always rested on a delicate and easily shaken foundation, and there have always been danger zones—pirate coasts or frontier areas—beyond the law. Even supposedly stable societies at peace have not been spared men of political violence, assassins, vigilantes, and revolutionaries with their urgent dreams. Throughout history, piracy and revolution, sometimes with official sponsorship, have disrupted the international order.

Under the influence of ethical ideals and practical incentives, a remarkable amount of progress has been made toward securing transnational relationships and establishing a single world under law. However, as the world has become increasingly interdependent, it has become more vulnerable to assault. Increasingly the custodians of order in an era of détente have been faced with violent assaults by men who seek to punish the transnational system for, as they see it, denying them justice. The transnational terrorist sees order as oppression and stability as tyranny disguised and is apparently beyond reconciliation through accommodation or control through the power of conventional force.

Such men and such violent and spectacular acts are hardly novel. The spoor of the terrorist, however defined, can be found throughout history. Often terror serves the state as well as the rebel, as in 1595 when Ottoman Sultan Mohammed killed his nineteen brothers to eliminate dynastic competitors or more recently when the Ku Klux Klan vigilantes defended a threatened system in the American South.

Still, attention has usually focused on the lone assassin or the tiny band of conspirators. Such men have taken victims from all cultures and eras—presidents, tsars, kings and, on the eve of World War I, an archduke. Some, like the IMRO organization which sought to link Macedonia to Bulgaria, operated across national boundaries. Others

4

concentrated on eliminating a single tyrant or punishing an individual traitor.

If there has been in modern times an archetypal terrorist organization dedicated to revolutionary violence, the People's Will *(Narodynaya Volya)* of tsarist Russia most nearly qualifies, primarily because its members, unlike many other revolutionaries, fashioned and advocated a philosophy of "personal terror." Russian populists, frustrated by their efforts to organize an indifferent peasantry, harassed by the tsarist police, and determined on radical change, met secretly in 1879, forming the People's Will and deciding upon a strategy of terror. The People's Will evolved as a small, dedicated, and tightly disciplined complex of regional cells, a classic underground resistance movement. Even before the group was formed there were scattered individual assassination attempts, and during 1879, in April and November, there were actually two attempts on the tsar's life. In the second episode a bomb in the Winter Palace killed ten guards and wounded fifty-three other people. Ultimately, in March 1881, the People's Will killed Tsar Alexander II by detonating a bomb under his sled.

These Russian radicals were early reaching the theoretical stage, but they did not remain alone in advocating personal terror. The tiny People's Will, with in 1881 perhaps as few as fifty activists and certainly not more than five hundred, became a model for many others, particularly the revolutionary anarchists, who would rely on a strategy of assassination for over a generation. Various theoreticians—Nicolas Morozov, Johann Most, Serge Nechayev, and Mikhail Bakunin—were studied assiduously, though now they are known only to specialists. The most extreme of these was Nechayev, who wrote *Revolutionary Catechism* that for many epitomizes the philosophy of personal terror. Consider his characterization of the revolutionary:

> The revolutionary is a dedicated man. He has no personal inclinations, no business affairs, no emotions, no attachments, no property, and no name. Everything in him is subordinated towards a single exclusive attachment, a single thought, and a single passion—the revolution. . . . he has torn himself away from the bonds which tie him to the social order and to the cultivated world, with all its laws, moralities, and customs. . . . The revolutionary despises public opinion . . . morality is everything which contributes to the triumph of the revolution. Immoral and criminal is everything that stands in his way. . . . Night and day he must have but one thought, one aim—

5

merciless destruction . . . he must be ready to destroy himself and destroy with his own hands everyone who stands in his way.[5]

Never mind that Nechayev founded only fantasy organizations and never became involved in a serious revolutionary deed. Although he himself was in fact not taken very seriously, his "catechism" has for many described the terrorist perfectly. The terrorist act is not so easily described.

Terror: The Definitional Problem. If, as was demonstrated by the unproductive UN deliberations in 1973 and the postponements of further discussion in 1974, there is no satisfactory political definition of terror extant or forthcoming, there is similarly no common academic consensus as to the essence of terror and no common language with which to shape a model acceptable to political scientists or social psychologists. Terror appears to be a condition known implicitly to most men, but which is somehow beyond rigorous examination. A student of violence cannot test his theories through controlled laboratory experimentation. For while it seems obvious that the threat or reality of danger may produce certain psychological responses in the potential victim, the numerous variables involved preclude useful generalization. Furthermore, no debilitating effects—fright, stress, or anguish—need necessarily result from every act of terror. This is particularly true when the act of terror is aimed at a strong individual leader. Repeated assassination attempts against men as different as Charles de Gaulle and King Hussein of Jordan apparently effected no change in their politics or their personalities. Remarkably, even in areas of interest and continual danger from terrorist activities, most people continue their normal rounds, undoubtedly under stress, and perhaps in considerable turmoil, but not in any visible way "in the grip of terror." The individual and collective psychological response to violent coercion is so unpredictable and subject to so many variables that it would be futile to focus on it.

Of course, the difficulties of academicians in parsing rigorous, verifiable results concerning the responses of the victims of a campaign of violence has not inhibited the practitioners of such a strategy, who continue to assume that the arbitrary violence will maintain a desirable

---

[5] Serge Nechayev, *Revolutionary Catechism*, quoted in David C. Rapoport, *Assassination and Terrorism* (Toronto: Canadian Broadcasting Corporation, 1971), p. 79.

climate of intimidation. But the terrorist is interested in his victim's response only to the extent that it helps him obtain his goals. Thus the efficacy of each act of terrorism can be most effectively judged on the basis of the professed intentions of its perpetrator and the verifiable political results of the act. This study will, therefore, emphasize not the suffering of the victim, but the nature of the violent act and the intentions of those responsible.

Even this restricted approach leaves open the question of which deeds to include. Legitimate regimes threatened with any sort of revolutionary violence swiftly denounce all violent opponents as terrorists, but the revolutionary contends that state violence is nothing more than *authorized* terror. Moreover, under certain circumstances, ostensibly terrorist acts have come to possess a certain legitimacy. Uninvolved observers tend to agree that there has been recourse to terror when the operation avoids accepted military techniques in favor of assassination, kidnapping, and air hijacking. Such revolutionary tactics are readily recognizable as variants of criminal acts and are often wanton or random in application.

The operations of uniformed guerrillas have gradually been accepted as an unconventional but recognized form of war. When guerrilla tactics and techniques are brought into urban areas to be used by men without uniforms and endangering innocent civilians, the distinction between unconventional war and terror becomes less clear, even when the guerrillas seek to maintain a military image. Guerrilla war, urban or rural, may well expand in brutal and unacceptable ways, in violation of any accepted norm and limited only by revolutionary or governmental expediency. Beyond the catch-all umbrella term "guerrilla war," revolutionary or state terror operations cannot really be described in military terms at all. In the eyes of most, terrorism is monstrous and could only be the work of irrational fanatics.

Sometimes the public finds terror unacceptable even when it is the more merciful alternative. Few of the uninvolved want to be told that the judicious murder of scores of Vietnamese headmen might be a more effective and humane technique for controlling the countryside than the indiscriminate use of B-52s. In America, after the trauma of the last decade, few can view assassination dispassionately as a merciful means to effect change in areas where conventional politics might engender more widespread violence. Somehow the demonstrable horrors of war seem pale in contrast to the unbridled use of dreadful means by

7

nameless men without moderation. This is natural, for terrorists often intentionally cultivate a general response of horror. Terror may strike only one victim, yet have many vicarious targets. The murder of one policeman may be intended to intimidate an entire police force.

The practitioners of terror can largely be catagorized on the basis of their aspirations, although tidy academic categories readily become blurred when applied to real-life situations. For example, some psychotics find the appeal of revolutionary organizations so strong that they mimic revolutionary violence. But as most such persons have a long history of social alienation and failure, they are often unable to relate satisfactorily to others and therefore make poor candidates for viable professional revolutionary movements requiring disciplined dedication. The criminal also may drift on the violent edge of revolution— attracted by the decay of civil order—but few criminals possess the talents needed for an armed struggle. There can be no doubt, however, that from time to time hysterical men performing acts easily defined as criminal will rationalize their deed with political verbiage.

Patho-Politics: Cathartic Violence. In New York City in 1973, two police patrolmen, one white and one black, were gunned down in the East Village in a particularly brutal and apparently senseless act of murder. Two days later United Press International received a "Black Liberation Army" letter of explanation that ended with the warning that "there is more to come." This new black terrorist group had evolved out of the splintered remains of the Black Panthers and was not really an organization, but rather a collection of tiny, fluid groups of militants continually merging and dissolving. Though these men did not operate transnationally, their style derived from the transnational model, and their politics reflected the influence of third-world revolutionary theory. Often recruited to black nationalism in prison, they had drifted on the edge of events while living on the proceeds of theft and robbery. Partially educated or self-taught, they had become outlaws even from the black ghetto. The Black Liberation Army consisted of these violent outcasts of the urban jungle, driven by hatred of the system and outraged at their own limited prospects. Having absorbed the contemporary political language of revolution, they claimed that the system had destroyed them, that the prisons, not the prisoners, were at fault. For these murderous, frustrated blacks, the Black Liberation Army was not so much a revolutionary conspiracy as an acceptable self-rationale for violent revenge

8

against authority. And for these driven men, the most visible pillar of the system was the police. They saw any patrolman, whether black or white, only as a blue target—the enemy.

An even more bizarre "revolutionary movement," again domestic in operation but transnational in orientation, surfaced in California in 1973 when the "Symbionese Liberation Army" (SLA) claimed responsibility for the murder of Oakland Superintendent of Schools Marcus Foster. After two suspects were arrested (both of whom were subsequently convicted on first-degree murder charges), the nature of the movement began to become clear to authorities. Founded in June 1973, the SLA was part cult and part ultra-radical conspiracy. It was comprised of a few dozen men and women, both black and white, coming from diverse backgrounds—university rebels, escaped convicts, and drifters. Their leader, "Cinque," a self-styled general field marshal, would later state in a taped message that "we are savage killers and madmen . . . willing to give our lives to free the people at any cost." [6] (General Field Marshal Cinque was Donald DeFreeze, a thirty-year-old escaped black convict.) In February 1974, Cinque became known to the nation when the SLA kidnapped Patricia Hearst, granddaughter of the late William Randolph Hearst.

The first SLA communication after the kidnapping, a patchwork letter filled with revolutionary jargon and rhetoric, warned that "should any attempt be made by authorities to rescue the prisoner or to arrest or harm any SLA element, the prisoner is to be executed." [7] The Hearst family, with the cooperation of the FBI, attempted to placate the SLA.

The first demand was for free food for all people receiving welfare or Social Security or participating in food-stamp programs. The cost of such an initial "good faith" program would be, officials estimated, $239 million. The SLA seemed to have little understanding of the problem of distributing the food or the scope of their demand. The Hearsts eventually put up $2 million, agreeing to fund additional food distribution if Patricia were released. Subsequently, communication with the kidnappers became sporadic and then seemed to break down, when to the amazement of all, on 3 April Patricia Hearst sent a tape to her parents announcing her "conversion" to the SLA.

This kidnapping, like the murder of Marcus Foster, turned out to have only the most marginal political content. The Hearsts' repeated

---

[6] *New York Times*, 8 February 1974.

[7] *Washington Post*, 13 February 1974.

9

pleas over television increasingly took the tone of psychiatric sessions, plea bargaining with the demented, whose erratic actions progressively belied their political rhetoric.

The final act in the bizarre SLA "revolution" was a spectacular shoot-out in Los Angeles between most of the SLA members and a tactical squad of the city police. America watched on color television as the SLA went up in flames. When the battle ended, only Patty Hearst and two other SLA members were left at large. The SLA war against "the Fascist Capitalist Class and all their agents of murder, oppression and exploitation" [8] had consisted of the murder of a black school official, the kidnapping of a nineteen-year-old girl (which precipitated a haphazard distribution of several million dollars worth of food), a flawed bank robbery, and a tragicomic shoplifting attempt.

Such "rebels" reveal the hazards of categorization and the hazy boundary dividing the committed revolutionary from the violent eccentric. The sort of driven men and women as made up the memberships of the SLA and the Black Liberation Army exist on the margin of rationality and can only function by resort to a violence that is ultimately self-destructive.

The Varieties of Terror

Psychotic. The term "abnormal behavior," like terror, has continually defied satisfactory definition. Still, it is clear that those who attempt bizarre, ostensibly political actions with uncertain or irrational outward motivations do so for what are internal, personal reasons. American society has recently witnessed several examples of a particular variant of deviant behavior, that of the psychotic assassin. A distressing number of Americans make and/or attempt to carry out threats against significant political figures, particularly the President. While the assassin's profile is well known—he or, as the blundered attempt on President Gerald Ford in September 1975 revealed, she usually is the product of a broken home, has serious sexual problems, has a history of frequent unemployment, and is incapable of establishing effective personal relationships—it is all too common to be of practical use. Even a few thousand such potential psychotic assassins in a nation of more than 200 million would defy the capabilities of the Secret Service.

---

[8] *New York Times*, 12 February 1974.

With the exception of the attack by the National Party of Puerto Rico on President Harry S. Truman in 1950 and perhaps the conspiracy against Lincoln, all significant American assassination attempts have been by psychotics who rationalized their act with the language of politics. Guiseppe Zangara, who killed Mayor Anton Cermak of Chicago while attempting to assassinate President Franklin Roosevelt, claimed that hatred of kings and presidents was his motivation, while Sirhan Sirhan claims to have killed Robert Kennedy out of love for Palestine. In the nineteenth century, an attempt on the life of Andrew Jackson was made by a destitute house painter who claimed to be Richard III of England. Perhaps only Arthur Bremer, the disturbed young man without friends or prospects who shot Governor George Wallace of Alabama, did not pretend a political motive. He sought recognition only—better to be wanted for murder than not wanted at all—and became a violent footnote to history. After the act it was easy to fit the psychotic-assassin profile to Bremer, but America is crowded with men like Bremer, men who will live lives of lonely desperation without being driven to express their hostility through violence.

Those who would act out their fantasies by murdering the mighty are only one variant in the pool of psychotics whose acts can threaten transnational order. The appeal of skyjacking airliners—the power of command and the prospect of capture—has attracted a certain type of deviant. In this particular case, the recognizable profile of the potential skyjacker coupled with the constraints of boarding an airplane made an early warning system reasonably effective.

Still, from time to time a skyjacker will slip through the net. In August 1973, for example, Mohammed Touni, a Libyan citizen with a history of mental problems, hijacked a Lebanese jet to Tel Aviv "to bring peace" to the Middle East. And on 22 February 1974, an unemployed salesman who had previously been committed to a Philadelphia hospital for mental observation and twice had been arrested for picketing the White House, killed a guard and a pilot in a bungled attempt to seize an airliner at the Baltimore airport and crash it into the White House. Later that year, the White House was similarly threatened, by a helicopter assault and then by a fake human bomb.

Such violent and irrational behavior follows fashions and cycles. In France, for example, a Lille high school student burned himself to death "to protest the situation in Biafra," setting off a particularly gruesome cycle of self-immolations that soon reached a total of fourteen.

Presumably then, whatever novel and spectacular deeds are devised in the future by the true terrorist, a few of the demented will mimic them.

Criminal. Air piracy has been one of the most common manifestations of this variant of terror. The peculiar attraction of skyjacking for strictly criminal purposes was its simplicity. One not necessarily bright man with a gun could commandeer a highly expensive getaway vehicle, ask for a large ransom, and then fly off to sanctuary. Without sanctuary the getaway jet had no value except to a trained parachutist, of which, fortunately, there were few in the criminal world. Once the risks of capture before the act had been vastly increased by preventive measures and the risks of imprisonment after the act had become almost certain, air piracy became less attractive to the criminal. In the United States, for example, there were no successful skyjackings in 1973, and one failure at Baltimore on 22 February 1974. The last successful American attempt was in November 1972, when three gunmen took over a Southern Airways jet and embarked on a harrowing nine-stop, twenty-nine-hour odyssey that finally ended in Havana. By 1975, there was only one successful case still outstanding of skyjacking for ransom. As with train robbery, prevention techniques had largely caught up with the criminal, if not with the psychopath.

There are fashions in crime as well as in deviant behavior, and the history of air piracy demonstrates that the criminal, like the deviate, will mimic others' tactics. This would seem to explain the recent surge in kidnappings. If international companies are willing to pay vast sums to Argentine guerrillas to use "for the people" or in pursuit of the revolution, then kidnapping for profit in Argentina or elsewhere becomes a highly lucrative business. In Italy kidnapping and extortion became particularly popular after the reported ransom of $2.8 million paid in the kidnapping of J. Paul Getty III. This in turn has caused a boom in the bodyguard business.

The SLA combined aspects of the Getty kidnapping in Italy with the tactics of the Argentine guerrillas for their own "political" purposes, and a married couple in Atlanta quickly mimicked the scenario for simple criminal purposes, kidnapping the editor of the *Atlanta Constitution* in the name of the "American Revolutionary Army." (Both were arrested almost at once and the $700,000 ransom seized.) By then a rash of kidnappings was underway. Under adult instruction, teenagers on Long Island seized a young boy, only to be rounded up immediately on his

12

release. A banker's wife was kidnapped in Minneapolis, as was another man in Florida. Within less than two months the FBI was involved in a dozen cases—and American insurance companies quietly began selling kidnapping insurance.

Endemic. There are some societies bounded by national borders where the only law is that of the strong. Anarchy flourishes amid tribal massacre, blood feuds, and parochial quarrels often disguised with ideological rhetoric or carried out in the name of an entrenched regime. In a country like Amin's Uganda there is no certainty that international flights can land or take off with impunity, that aliens can count on protection, or that the conventions of diplomacy will be respected or even recognized. That such chaos benefits no one, least of all the outlaw regime itself, often means little to a threatened elite with inherited hatreds or to a primitive despot. Economic development, international respect, order, and law may be secondary priorities.

In many cases such a collapse into barbarism and endemic terror will not greatly concern the international community as long as trade patterns can be adjusted. When suddenly a substantial portion of the world supply of an important commodity can no longer be shipped through or from a particular nation wracked by internal disorder, the problem may become more serious. By and large, however, the general response to endemic terror has been to avoid the danger zone.

Authorized. Over the years there has arisen a set of conventions concerning the use of state power for coercive purposes. This has been particularly true with regard to war between nations and in some cases even for civil war. These rules of war, whether incorporated in the Geneva Convention or in various treaties and agreements, were developed because they are universally advantageous, although this of course has not prevented repeated violations. The rules forbid the deliberate killing of civilians, the torture of prisoners, and the use of poison gas. They further stipulate that aggression is never to be rewarded. When the rules are broken, rationalizations, charges and counter-charges, and at times even criminal proceedings, follow.

The rules are flexible and open to "adjustment." In the case of Hiroshima and Nagasaki, Americans contend that American lives had been saved, which is undoubtedly true, and that, on balance, Japanese lives were saved as well, which may be true, but it is difficult to imagine

13

many prewar Americans who could have sanctioned the total destruction of an entire city as a legitimate act of war. Whether or not such military operations can be defined as terror is to a degree immaterial during a war situation, for then the fabric of international order has been so badly rent, even by conventional operations, that definitions are of little importance. War, no matter what the techniques, disturbs transnational order, and conventional wars with approved means do so more easily and directly than revolutionary terror.

Some regimes also authorize or at least employ techniques to maintain internal order that can be readily recognized by the distant observer as a form of terror: random purges, show trials, torture, internment. In some periods and nations such tactics appear systemic rather than a response to specific provocation. This use of terror for political control, as long as it remains internal, may in no way disturb trade patterns, foreign investment, or treaty obligations.

A regime may authorize the pursuit of dissidents beyond its own national boundaries—as when Trotsky was struck down with an ice ax in Mexico, when White Russians were abducted in Paris, or when Ukrainian nationalists were assassinated with gas guns in Germany. A most recent example of such a campaign is the Israeli response (assassinations throughout Europe and the Middle East) to the Palestinian fedayeen attacks.

Remarkably, such authorized terror on a transnational basis has rarely been employed. At least, there have been few highly visible or highly successful operations. Few leaders are anxious to organize the assassination of a rival, fearing the response. There have been exceptions, however, as the recent revelations about CIA assassination plots—if nothing more—reveal. The late Dominican President Rafael Trujillo encouraged attacks on President Rómulo Betancourt of Venezuela, and the long series of assassination attempts on King Hussein of Jordan has been directed, sponsored, or fostered by his various Arab enemies. Authorized terror across national boundaries does occur on occasion, and needless to say, it does little for the stability of international order.

Vigilante. Quite often a threatened regime may prefer that volunteers rush into the breach—without formal authorization—doing for the state what the state prefers to avoid doing itself. Thus, in Brazil, off-duty policemen murder "known" criminals, and in Guatemala groups such as *Ojo por Ojo* (Eye for an Eye) and *Mano Blanca* (White Hand) murder opponents of the regime with impunity. Mehdi Ben Barka and other Algerians were murdered by Frenchmen frustrated by legal restraints.

Certain vigilantes may operate to protect a society without the support of a recognized protective regime. Thus the Ku Klux Klan sought through violence and intimidation to avoid a radical reconstruction of Southern society. Random murder and arbitrary intimidation of blacks became a conventional part of rural Southern life.

In Northern Ireland, with the visible decay of the former system of Protestant predominance (capped by the suspension of the regional assembly at Stormont in 1972), an ill-organized but persistent campaign of random murder of Catholics was adopted for the preservation of "a Protestant state for a Protestant people." These murders are founded on hatred and fear—fear of the Catholic Church, of incorporation into a united "Papish" Ireland, and of the prospect of being "sold out" by London. Because the new Northern Ireland Assembly seemed determined on Catholic-Protestant accommodation, the response of the desperate Protestants was a resort not only to a general strike but also to violence with the hope of protecting the old ways. Once again, neither the Protestant gunman in Belfast nor the hooded member of the Ku Klux Klan in Alabama has any great effect on international order, for vigilantes are primarily committed to the preservation of an established domestic order, even as they violate the law of the land.

Revolutionary. This form of terror takes on several aspects which, though they often overlap, can best be examined separately.

Organizational terror. To the threatened, all revolutionaries are terrorists, guilty of using or planning to use coercive violence against a legitimate state. Unlike the People's Will, very few contemporary terrorists are willing to acknowledge their operations as terroristic; yet every revolutionary organization, perhaps without exception, must face the problem of maintaining internal discipline, inhibiting penetration, and punishing errant members. Such activity can be described as "organizational terror." To be most effective, punishment must be swift, harsh, and visible. It is therefore often highly formalized, with a trial, defense, sentence, and execution. From time to time, and for specific purposes, there has been recourse to torture. In 1941, for example, members of the Irish Republican Army (IRA) Council arrested the IRA chief of staff on the suspicion that he had been an agent of the Dublin government for some years. He was roughly handled until he "confessed." Then he was formally tried under IRA rules and sentenced to death. He evaded execution only by escape. Generally, internal organizational terror is not meant to intimidate others, but to punish the guilty. The assumption, even when demonstrably without basis, is that most of the revolutionary apples in the barrel are sound and that the cadres can trust each other even though vigilance must be maintained.

Allegiance terror. A less restrained variant of organizational terror is the revolutionaries' use of violence in order to create mass support. Such "support" in the form of funds may be obtained through extortion, while "support" in the form of right action—strikes, boycotts, spoiled ballots—may be obtained by threats of vengeance. In the case of the Algerian FLN in France, it appeared at times that the major organizational campaign rested firmly on a foundation of terror, which, if not random, was at least remarkably indiscriminate. Since at times many revolutionary organizations resort to acts of violence to maintain momentum and appease militants—as well as to pay the bills—there has been a tendency to assume that this is the *only* means open to such movements and that whatever support exists is coerced, not volunteered. The rebel responds that without state coercion, few would pay taxes, serve on a jury, or risk their lives in the conventional military.

Functional terror. Beyond organizational terror, a necessity for most rebels, lies "functional terror," which is employed when in the course of an armed struggle it is necessary to gain strategic advantage through specific action. In Ireland, on 21 November 1920 (Bloody Sunday) IRA squads descended on the safe-houses of sixteen British undercover agents in Dublin, killing them all and at a blow destroying the British intelligence net. The victims were specifically chosen because of their function.

Often, rather than choosing individual victims, revolutionary commanders will decide on a category of victims, for example, declaring any policeman who fails to resign a potential target. In a tightly organized insurrection in which the rebel maintains an interest in his image, there is a reluctance to broaden such target groups beyond the military or other uniformed services, but sometimes civilians may become targets.

At times the category of victims becomes vastly expanded. To the Popular Front for the Liberation of Palestine, *any* traveler who flies to Israel is fair game. In such circumstances, terror is effectively random. Clearly, the major *function* of spraying machine-gun fire into a transit lounge is not the elimination of the immediate victims, but rather the general intimidation of all potential visitors to Israel. In fact, it is rare when there is no broader impact even from the most discrete use of functional terror. As noted, the death of just one policeman may intimidate all his fellows, reveal the shakiness of a regime, and draw international attention. It may engender new support and stiffen old and have all sorts of spin-off benefits beyond the elimination of one man.

Provocative terror. As the distance grows between the specific victim and the larger objective, "provocative terror," which concentrates on exploiting the deed and escalating its impact, comes into play. For example, unintentionally, but not unexpectedly, when the IRA shot the British agents on Bloody Sunday in 1920—a specific act of functional terror—it provoked a response which led to a long-term readjustment of the political situation, which proved to be of much greater advantage than the immediate functional gain of eliminating spies. As part of the British reprisal, three IRA men, including the officer in command of Dublin, were picked up that same evening and shot "while trying to escape." This "authorized" murder of three IRA men might have passed muster in Britain—the lads had been sorely provoked by an IRA that murdered from the ditch. During the afternoon, however, a group of Black and Tans, an auxiliary military security force of dubious repute, had "spontaneously" fired into a crowd at a football game, killing twelve spectators and wounding sixty. This British public opinion could not accept. Ultimately, there arose a consensus in England that if Ireland could only be ruled through a policy of counterterror, in opposition to British traditions and wont, then it was not worth ruling at all. The IRA had provoked—unintentionally—the response which led to this advantageous shift in public opinion.

Of course, all targets at all levels do not respond to provocative terror in similar ways. What worked for the IRA and, later, in Palestine for the *Irgun Zvai Leumi* would hardly have been effective against a government less vulnerable to shifts in public opinion—for example, Nazi Germany or Communist Russia. No matter who the opponent, however, there remains an opportunity to exploit the deed beyond its discrete function through the technique of manipulation.

17

Manipulative terror. The most common use of this technique is the creation of a bargaining situation, in which the terrorists threaten to destroy seized assets or hostages unless they are granted certain demands. Manipulative terror rests on the dread, if not the certainty, that such threats are real. The anguish can be intensified by the visible hysteria of the terrorists and the confusion of the moment. Thus, manipulative terror extends the drama of the deed while it seeks a functional gain in terms of freed prisoners or ransom and *forces* the target to react in what are assumed to be advantageous ways. There may be spin-off benefits elsewhere if the public becomes delighted by the daring and audacity of the terrorists. If the public is horrified, the terrorist action may force people to ask why men would be driven to such actions.

Symbolic terror. Truly symbolic terrorism must go beyond the organizational and functional and must select as a victim a figure who represents the epitome of the enemy. Yet the deed must be more than simple vengeance. When in 1973 the Basque revolutionary movement *Euzkadi ta Azkatasuna* (ETA) assassinated Spanish Premier Luis Carrero Blanco, the larger target was Franco Spain and the system which denied Basque aspirations and institutionalized oppression. Given the regime's track record, there was no prospect of manipulating any advantageous Spanish response, for the action would only produce swift, rigorous, and brutal repression. Furthermore, the removal of that specific individual was of no particular strategic advantage to the ETA. Certainly, as is the case with any successful and effective terrorist act, the revolutionary morale improved and there were broad propaganda benefits, but the major returns were, and were intended to be, symbolic.

Similarly, when the *Organisation de l'Armée Secrète* (OAS) tried and repeatedly failed to assassinate Charles de Gaulle, they sought not simple vengeance—the death of the man who had betrayed a French Algeria—but a symbolic triumph over France itself. De Gaulle's death might not, as some had hoped, change history, but through it the OAS would have made history.

A key component of the more elaborate terrorist operations has been the capacity of the revolutionaries to orchestrate a violent drama, that is, to write in roles for the oppressor, extend the duration of the deed, and bargain on various levels. All this has been made possible by television and other news media which can give immediate and extensive coverage to the unfolding horror. The media can be manipulated to revolutionary advantage, coerced or encouraged to play the middleman, as was the case in the SLA Hearst kidnapping. Because the revolutionary seeks objectives beyond the immediate results of the actual deed, he must increase the impact through the horror of his actions. The Palestinian terrorist action at the Munich Olympics demonstrated how effectively terrorists can utilize the media to this end.[9] There can be little doubt that the international communications net is for any potential terrorist a new asset guaranteeing propaganda on a scale far beyond the imagination of the nineteenth-century revolutionary anarchists.

The Anatomy of a Revolutionary Terrorist Strategy: Lehi, Lord Moyne, and Bernadotte

Many spectacular terrorist deeds are of uncertain motive, hectic in orchestration, and of mixed results. There are so many variables, so few available articulate terrorists, and such a miasma of outraged indignation and shoddy rationalization surrounding the whole topic that there is seldom any valid analysis. It is possible in a few cases, however, to follow in detail and with some rigor specific terrorist operations which took place in a transnational medium, for transnational purpose, and with reasonably clear results.

Even after a generation, the activities of the Stern Group (Fighters for the Freedom of Israel, or Lehi) in the Middle East are readily recalled. Lehi, a tiny group of true Zionist believers, organized a series of ruthless, violent, and spectacular deeds that may actually have changed history and which, in any case, have left a record that can be examined with an eye to discovering the anatomy of transnational terror.[10]

In one form or another terror has long played a role, often a predominant one, in Middle Eastern politics. In much of this century, it has been particularly associated with the Zionist presence. Before the establishment of Israel, there had been massacres and riots as the

---

[9] When the Baader-Meinhof anarchists threatened a rocket attack on the East-West German World Cup soccer match in June 1974, they mimicked the Arabs' Munich tactic of selecting a stage that would guarantee attention. In this case the police carried out extensive raids in February to prevent any such "deed."

[10] A more elaborate analysis of the Stern Group's activities can be found in J. Bowyer Bell, "Assassination in International Politics, Lord Moyne, Count Bernadotte, and the Lehi," *International Studies Quarterly*, vol. 16, no. 1 (March 1972), pp. 59-82.

aspirations of the Zionists and the Arabs clashed. Between 1936 and 1939 the Arab revolt—part strike, part brigandage, and part irregular war—harassed the British, for whom the strategic benefits of their control of the Palestine Mandate still outweighed the cost of maintaining order. After 1939 and the outbreak of World War II, the British had assumed that the Zionist underground armies—the large militia-type Hagana, with the Palmach commandos, and the small schismatic and militant Irgun Zvai Leumi—would be quiescent, at least during the struggle against Hitler. In this the mandate authorities were wrong. The issue split Irgun, and a small group emerged under the leadership of Avraham Stern who, war or no, wanted to begin at once to create a Zionist state through armed struggle. Stern's group engaged in a series of provocative operations that led to gun fights in the streets. These ended in Stern's death in February 1942 ("while attempting to escape") and the apparent collapse of his movement. There the matter seemed to rest, with British attention focused on the war and Zionist aspirations in cold storage.

Stern's followers, however, did not despair. Yitshak Yizernitsky-Shamir escaped from the Mazra Detention Camp and began to build Lehi with an original base of a few dozen members. With him in a three-man high command were Nathan Friedman Yellin-Mor, a propagandist, tactician, and political organizer who had escaped from Latrun Detention Camp in October 1942, and Yisrael (Scheib) Eldad, an expert on Schopenhauer who became the charismatic and visionary ideologist of the group. Despite their vision, hard work, and organization, by the beginning of 1943 Lehi numbered only a hundred or so members, a quite insufficient base for an insurrection or even a guerrilla campaign of attrition. Lehi thus chose to follow a strategy of individual terror. While the Lehi leadership, largely from Eastern Europe, was familiar with the theorists of terror, the ideas of Stern dominated the movement and determined in large part its particular terrorist strategy. Stern had placed no faith in the moderate elders of Zionism and had even mistrusted his colleagues in Irgun, for he held that only by force could the British be driven from Zion. Stern had insisted that acts would educate and, more specifically, that acts of terror would enlighten not only the British but also the overly cautious Jewish population of Palestine, who were too fearful of British wrath and too dedicated to restraint. Stern's campaign, however, had collapsed in a series of retaliatory police actions with little symbolic and no manipulative value. The high com-

20

mand of Lehi thus determined to seek more appropriate victims and a broader target.

The prime focus of Lehi attention was British High Commissioner Sir Harold MacMichael, who, following his instructions from London, had "closed the gates" and continued to limit Jewish immigration into the mandate despite the European holocaust. As a symbol of the closed gates and the oppressing power in Palestine, Lehi believed MacMichael would be a most suitable victim. The group made five abortive attempts before MacMichael was slightly wounded in an ambush on 8 August 1944. Lehi then decided—since MacMichael was due to be recalled to Britain by the end of the month—to move up what had been planned as a second more grave and decisive action—the assassination of Lord Moyne, British minister of state in Cairo.

Lehi assumed that by undertaking such an operation in Cairo they would educate not only the British and the Jews, but also the Arabs, who, as similar victims of British imperialism, shared a common enemy with the Zionists. Lehi's leaders believed that Moyne's assassination would help the world understand that the dispute in Palestine was not a disagreement between a local administration and the Zionist "natives," but a fundamental cleavage between the rightful heirs to Palestine and an alien British imperial presence. The future of Zion thereafter could not be quietly adjusted to British convenience. Britain, and Moyne's successor, would have to consider the cost of enforcing any anti-Zionist policy. And, more importantly, through this deed Lehi would gain a forum to argue the merits of Zionist aspirations, for their action would internationalize the Palestine issue. Failing to so act, Lehi could not negotiate in conventional ways and could not attract support or oppose enemies even by irregular war. Their only option was recourse to symbolic terror. And in Cairo on 6 November 1944, Lord Moyne became Lehi's victim when two young men shot and killed him outside the British Residency.

The immediate general reaction was horror and indignation. The Jewish Agency was stunned at the "revolting crime." Prime Minister Winston Churchill, long thought to be pro-Zionist, told the House of Commons that Britain might have to reconsider support of a Jewish homeland. The Egyptians were fearful they would be blamed, and no one had a kind word for the "fanatics" responsible. Even Irgun, engaged since January 1944 in its own limited armed struggle against the British, had grave doubts about the wisdom of such a deed. Who would gain?

The British were angry; the Arabs fearful; the Zionists in Palestine still more fearful. The two assassins were swiftly tried and convicted, and on 23 March 1945 they were executed. They explained, "Our deed stemmed from our motives, and our motives stemmed from our ideals, and if we prove our ideals are right and just, then our deed was right and just." [11] Few were convinced then or later, except those in Lehi, who felt that the course of history *had* been changed—that their act had made a viable Jewish resistance possible, internationalized the Palestine issue, and alerted British and world opinion.

Over the next four years Lehi, and to a degree Irgun, would continue to try channeling the flow of history by violent deeds others deplored. To a great many, again including most Zionists, the most deplorable Lehi action of all was the assassination of United Nations Mediator Count Folke Bernadotte. In Jerusalem on 17 September 1948 four men in Israeli army uniforms stopped Bernadotte's car. One thrust a Schmeisser submachine gun through the window and emptied the magazine; both Bernadotte and his aide, Colonel André Pierre Serot, were killed almost instantly. The four assassins disappeared, never to be apprehended. The next day an obscure organization called the Fatherland Front claimed credit, but everyone knew that Lehi had been responsible. The deed had too many earmarks of its tactics of personal terror.

The decision to assassinate Bernadotte had to a great extent resulted from a transformation that occurred within Lehi after the end of the underground struggle against the British and the beginning of open war against the Arabs during 1948. As it had become increasingly clear that the boundaries of Israel would be determined by conventional forces and not by revolutionaries, Lehi found that its part in the Zionist struggle would be small.

After June 1948, all Lehi soldiers had been integrated into the new Israeli Defense Force, except in beseiged Jerusalem. There appeared to be no way that Lehi could independently act on events, and no clear role for it in the future, once the foreign occupier had evacuated the mandate and the state of Israel had been declared. Lehi still wanted Israel to have territory on both sides of the Jordan—all, not part, of the Promised Land—but how a tiny group of zealots could assure the annexation of land completely in Arab hands escaped the imagination of even the most visionary. Even Lehi's cadres outside Jerusalem were controlled by

---

[11] G. Frank, *The Deed* (New York: Ballantine, 1963), p. 261.

others. The days of the underground were over. Some foresaw a conventional political role, others the absolute end to Lehi, but all the commanders agreed that before the situation became static Israel should have at least some additional territory and most assuredly it should have Jerusalem. Predictably, the hawkish Lehi commanders had little faith in the will or determination of the new Israeli cabinet of Premier David Ben-Gurion or in the generosity of the international community. For Lehi the appointment of Bernadotte suggested the prospect of an international "arrangement" not to Zionist advantage, an arrangement that the fearful Ben-Gurion might accept.

When Bernadotte arrived in the Middle East, apparently authorized to devise a "solution," the implication was clear that such a solution would be largely his alone and would then be imposed with international backing. Both the Israelis and Arabs assumed that they would somehow be forced to accept a solution, for no one foresaw decades of "no-war-no-peace." In June 1948, Bernadotte first suggested awarding much of the Negev and Jerusalem to Transjordan, and Western Galilee to Israel. The Israeli success in the renewed fighting during the summer produced no modification in his intentions. Serious discussion of the "Bernadotte problem" began within the Lehi high command in September. Lehi believed that Bernadotte had actually cooperated with the Nazis during the war and, more to the point, that assassination would simultaneously remove the Mediator and his Plan, while revealing the inability of the international community to intervene successfully in Israeli affairs. They also hoped such an act would stiffen the timorous Israeli cabinet. In Lehi's eyes Bernadotte had become a new symbol of the alien oppressor, intent on the implementation of a pro-Arab British policy. With the decision to assassinate Bernadotte, Lehi had again found a role. Again, it could act on events and, it was thought, change the course of history. And so the Lehi team assassinated Bernadotte. This was the last Lehi operation, for the deed destroyed Lehi, leaving it once more without a role.

The Lehi commanders have since contended that this final stroke terminated Bernadotte's plan, which proved to be the case, forced the Ben-Gurion cabinet to annex Jerusalem, which is probably not the case, and immunized Israel from any future international pressure since there had been no response to the deed beyond general indignation, which to some degree may be true. With regard to this last point, the ease with which Bernadotte was forgotten and the waffling of the United Nations certainly encouraged Israeli hawks to ignore "world opinion" and any United Nations "mission" that might conflict with Israeli interests.

In retrospect it seems clear that in the long run, Bernadotte's plan could hardly have been imposed on Israel, because while David Ben-Gurion might have been cautious, his Zionist dream definitely included both the Negev and Jerusalem. The deaths of Bernadotte and Moyne became the foundation for subsequent events; however, these events would very likely have occurred anyway. Lehi did not really change the long-run course of history, but it did accelerate the pace of events.

The two assassinations by Lehi, both almost classical exercises in personal terror, reveal most of the characteristics of such action. Terror was chosen by Lehi in 1944 out of weakness and the need for a spectacular event to expand the role of the organization. In 1948 it was a response to a different kind of weakness: the loss of direction. Both operations were rationally structured, and subsequent events evolved to the satisfaction of those responsible. In neither case was there hysteria or spontaneity; instead there was a cold, ruthless decision to alter a political situation by recourse to violence. Lehi's leaders believed that even if all their calculations were in error, only two men would have died in vain. Now, a generation later, the Lehi commanders, who have since taken bitterly opposing roads and rarely or never speak to each other, all still believe that Moyne and Bernadotte did not die in vain.

It must be emphasized that few terrorist deeds have the elegance and logic of those of Lehi, for however distressing and dreadful any assassination must be, the Lehi drama remains open to rational analysis. Other more haltingly crafted spectaculars are not so easily parsed. The lines between authorized terror and sponsored revolution are often vague, as are distinctions between random and discrete functional terror. Even the impact of an isolated insurrection on world order is difficult to weigh.

To the uneasy observer, the ostensibly terrorist acts of the demented are at least explicable. And for the optimist there is a potential remedy. The criminal has always been with us, and for him, too, there are conventional responses. There has always been distaste for regimes that resort to internal terror, but a remarkable toleration for them and even for authorized terror in the international medium as long as the operators are discreet. It is the new terrorists, slaughtering innocents in a transit lounge or hijacking jet airplanes, who cause the most concern, for such revolutionary terror seems a gruesome and unnecessary exercise in brutality that is counterproductive to the terrorists' stated aims.

While authorized terror in response to provocation seeks to impose a renewed order even if by illicit means, the revolutionary terrorist foments chaos, shaping momentary anarchy to his advantage. Willing to accept the disproportionate risks that would repel the criminal and capable of organization beyond the capacity of the demented, the transnational terrorist has gained a reputation as the new monster of the international medium. In today's world, even with its limited strategic role in revolutionary strategy, terror has often had a tremendous impact in insurrectional dramas throughout the world. But not all revolutionaries are terrorists, and not all terrorists are monsters. The guardians of order, therefore, must come to understand the aspirations, limitations, and intentions of the contemporary revolutionaries.

2

The Practitioners of Revolution

The Irish Republican Movement: Tradition and Techniques

In a world abounding with revolutionary organizations and armed struggles of every description, even the industrialized and supposedly stable Western democracies are at times beset by the violence of such groups as the Breton Liberation Front or the Irish Republican Army. To be sure, given the record of the past generation, most revolutionaries face a dim future. Few will succeed, especially now that the old and vulnerable colonial targets are gone. Still, who would have predicted that an original base of twelve young men hiding out in the Sierra Maestra could bring a successful revolution to Cuba? Rebels by their very nature must be optimistic, and in the beginning only the faithful few will realize that there is no alternative to rebellion but continued humiliation and thus accept the disproportionate risks. Often the hopeful rebel will find as his reward prison, exile, or despair, and these only if he does not find death first. Their hopes shattered, their cause in disarray, the would-be revolutionaries become defeated witnesses to the power of the system, for the center usually holds. None have so often and for so long a time sought the grail with the gun as have the Irish. An examination of the repeated and agonizing futility of their experience will yield a valuable insight into the revolutionary mind.

1798–1944. The Irish Republican movement, arising out of a confluence of the ideas of the French Revolution and the more ancient aspirations of Irish nationalism, has with all but monotonous regularity engendered armed rebellion against the British, the never-failing source of all Irish political evils. Since the 1798 rebellion the Irish Republicans have been dedicated to the principles of their founding father Wolfe Tone: "To unite the whole people of Ireland, to abolish the memory of all past dissensions and to substitute the common name of Irishmen in the place of the denomination of Protestant, Catholic, and Dissenter." [1]

Militant Republicans have remained faithful to Tone's essential objective, breaking the connection with Britain by physical force. While every generation has seen some Republicans siphoned off into politics, each has also retained its purists, the hard men who opt for physical force. The result has been the Irish "patriot game," a litany of violence, insurrection, assassinations, revolts, risings and guerrilla campaigns: 1798, 1803, 1848–1849, 1867, 1884, 1916, 1921, and continuing to the present day. The years are studded with the names of glory and defeat: the United Irishmen of 1798, the Young Irelanders in 1848, the Irish Republican Brotherhood after that, and the Fenians in the 1880s. And there is the litany of the martyrs: Tone, dead by his own hand, "Bold Robert Emmet" on the gallows tree, the Manchester Martyrs in 1884, Patrick Pearse and James Connolly and the other leaders of the Easter Rising in 1916, Terence McSweeney, who died on a hunger strike during the Tan War, and Barnes and McCormack, executed in England during the bombing campaign of the 1940s. There are ballads for Kevin Barry, hanged by the British, and Charlie Kerins, "The Boy from Tralee," hanged by the Irish. Desperate rebels in other countries may have to borrow from a distant tradition or seek idols from other struggles and other lands, but not so in Ireland, where the rebel staggers under his heritage and assumes a legitimacy denied by his opponents, the defenders of order.

Irish Republican history, largely a chronicle of failure, contains almost the entire spectrum of revolutionary strategy and tactics, including those beyond the narrow tradition of physical force: boycotts, civil disobedience campaigns, and even the conventional maneuvers of electoral politics. Often the Irish rebel seizes from his past strategies inappropriate for the present—the bomb when the ballot might work or a rural guerrilla campaign when the streets cry for demonstrators—but if he errs, the Irish Republican Army volunteer nonetheless acts within a legacy, conscious of his revolutionary ancestors and his historic responsibility. His act is not without reason, although it may prove

---

[1] For a detailed background, see J. Bowyer Bell, *The Secret Army, The IRA 1916-1970* (Cambridge: M.I.T. Press, 1974). *Cf.* T. P. Coogan, *The IRA* (New York: Praeger, 1970).

counterproductive to the cherished aim. It may well endanger the lives of the innocent, for a historical legacy has legitimized violence. Few rebels elsewhere can act within such a long historical tradition as the Irish, but most share the sense of the Irish insurgents that they are soldiers of destiny.

For nearly two centuries the Irish volunteer has found success just beyond the reach of one aborted campaign after another. By 1916 it appeared that politics had weakened the old Irish resolve, until a small band of militants rose in Dublin during Easter week. As usual, the uprising (this one known as the Easter Rising) failed, with the leaders executed and order restored. But this time the example would inspire a more pragmatic generation. By 1920 the ensuing Tan War had made Ireland, largely ungovernable by any means except coercion, so violent as to be unpalatable to British public opinion.[2] With guerrilla columns in the country and gunmen in the cities, and with the Royal Irish Constabulary demoralized, the IRA still could not expel the British or establish a counter-state, but neither could the British restore order. Ultimately negotiations led to the Anglo-Irish Treaty of 1921 that provided an intricate formula for the devolution of power to Dublin. There was to be an Irish Free State in the South, a special Northern Ireland province of Great Britain in the Northeast, and various other guarantees of British interests.

Despite the arguments of the Free Staters that Ireland had gained more than at any time in the previous 800 years, the militant Republicans refused to accept a treaty which specified partition and an oath to the crown and failed to establish the Republic. The result was a bitter civil war between the purist IRA and the new Free State government. Upon its defeat, the IRA went underground in May 1923. Shortly thereafter, seeing no hope of a military or a political victory, the long-time Republican leader Eamon De Valera abandoned the IRA militarists and the Sinn Fein abstentionists and sought to establish the Republic by conventional political means with his new Fianna Fail party. For a short while after De Valera came to power in 1932, the leadership of the IRA hoped to gain the Republic through an alliance with Fianna Fail.

---

2 Even in retrospect, it is a bit difficult to discover what the IRA Army Council really believed would happen—even under the best of circumstances—as a result of setting off many small bombs in British cities. Their "strategic" plan was obviously quite beyond the capacities of the IRA; the need to act certainly dominated all considerations, and only minimal thought was given to the potential result of any act.

Instead De Valera offered concessions which eroded IRA strength. With the transformation of the Free State into a truly independent Ireland in 1938, though still without the six counties of Ulster, the IRA had split and decayed and the hard men had grown desperate.

In 1938 a new Army Council was elected by the IRA Convention, and it embarked on a bombing campaign to force the British to grant Republican demands. The IRA bombs that went off in British cities in 1939 and 1940 caused only general indignation and a swift and effective response by British security forces. In Ireland the IRA's German contacts alarmed the neutral Dublin government, already dismayed by IRA violence in the South, and resulted in repression and internment, a policy that had been followed with vigor in the North since 1938. Eventually the IRA found itself frustrated everywhere and sapped by the scandal when its chief of staff was arrested and accused of treason by his own officers.[3] By 1944 the IRA had all but disappeared.

The Postwar Resurgence. After World War II, a few of the core members and some new recruits picked up the pieces and began again. This time the strategy was to wage a guerrilla campaign in the North and to avoid the futility of gunfights in the Dublin streets or bombs in London. Beginning with several spectacular arms raids on British army bases in 1954 and 1955, the IRA formally began the northern campaign in December 1956. Though there was some initial success, the Northern Ireland government was well prepared and the IRA had most limited resources. Support in the North began to dribble away and once more repression and internment were introduced in the South. In February 1962 the IRA Council finally recognized the inevitable and called off the campaign, ending sixteen years of work, planning and sacrifice. All told, the campaign had hardly been a major threat to the Northern Ireland regime—six policemen had been killed and thirty-two members of the security forces injured—although the fiscal cost of repression had been high. In any case, neither the London bombers nor the Ulster guerrillas had brought the Republic any closer.

After 1962, with the gun on the shelf, the Irish Republicans lacked direction and the capacity to act on events. Over the years the Dublin politicians had managed to transform the twenty-six southern counties into a viable Irish Republic, if not *the* Republic, thirty-two counties free and Gaelic as Tone had envisioned. During the same period the militant

[3] Bell, *The Secret Army.*

Republicans had only feuded among themselves or embarked on futile military adventures. Having alienated much of the Irish public, the IRA had become irrelevant to a modern Ireland no longer embroiled with the old issues and the old quarrels. If the formula provided by the Anglo-Irish Treaty was less than perfect, even in the eyes of the Dublin government, it seemed that it had at last brought an end to the ancient litany of rebellion. The prime minister from Stormont in Belfast and the Taoiseach (prime minister) from Leinster House in Dublin even exchanged visits. The fiftieth anniversary of the Easter Rising in 1966 had seen what was taken to be the last Republican hurrah, the bombing of Nelson's Pillar in Dublin. Actually, however, Ireland had reached the eve of new troubles that would revive the fortunes of the IRA, threaten the old treaty formula, and return the gun to Irish politics.

New Rumblings. In 1921 the British had assumed that in Northern Ireland the Protestant-loyalist community's distaste for an independent Ireland would provide a satisfactory foundation for dividing the island. At that time it might have been possible to work out the differences between North and South and by accommodation draw all Ireland closer to Great Britain, although perhaps at the expense of some Protestant protest. Instead, London turned Ulster over to the Protestants, who with a two-to-one majority fashioned a "Protestant state for a Protestant people." This intensified differences between all factions—North and South, Protestant and Catholic, and unionist and nationalist. The Protestants subjected the Catholic minority in Ulster to ritual humiliation. As much as possible, the unionist government at Stormont restricted the advantages of the partition to the Protestants. They added to the traditional prejudices—institutionalized injustices in voting, housing, employment, and welfare. All this occurred without any intervention by the British Parliament, which was delighted to be rid of the Irish issue for the first time in centuries. The IRA campaigns only convinced Stormont of the soundness of its anti-Catholic policy. For though rhetorical only, to Stormont the regular IRA demands for an end to partition from Dublin seemed a real threat. Thus since 1921 there had been no concessions to the Catholic nationalists, and from 1921 through the mid-1960s the Stormont regime had never been seriously challenged by Dublin, London, or the IRA.

The Stormont system first began to tremble in August 1968, when participants in a civil-rights demonstration—the first of its kind—

31

walked from Coalisland to Dungannon. Further such demonstrations increasingly alarmed Protestant loyalists who felt that these agitators represented the thin edge of the Catholic wedge and were legitimate protesters for the redress of real grievances. The largely Protestant police force had little sympathy for the demonstrators and reacted with predictable violence. But this time, the new generation of civil-rights militants, often led by university students, could not be beaten into submission. Repressive tactics could not be justified by writing off the dissidents as IRA men or Communist malcontents. This time the British public, watching the new Irish troubles on television, accepted the grievances as real and the protest as valid. Britain put pressure on Stormont for concessions that some feared would spark a violent Protestant backlash. As the Catholic minority became increasingly emboldened by success, it became willing to risk the traditional violence. The era of ritual humiliation had passed. First in Derry and then in Belfast widespread sectarian violence erupted.

Northern Ireland became a police state with too few police. In August 1969 London had to send the British army to contain the backlash by angry Protestant mobs. Wilson's Labour government somehow assumed that the presence of the army coupled with expressions of good intentions and the beginning of reform would ease the conflicts. As usual the British misjudged the Irish and ignored the dangers of maintaining an army as a police force in a community where recourse to violence had so frequently been the first choice of all parties.[4]

The Provo "Restoration." The Republican movement had from the first been attracted to the campaigns of civil disobedience and political agitation, realizing in 1968 and 1969 that guns posed a less viable threat to the Stormont system than banners in the street. The more militant and military Republicans gravely doubted the value of such political agitation and were apprehensive about the new IRA drift toward the left. The riots of August 1969 crystalized their opposition to this new direction. Seeking arms and men, northern IRA leaders, many ending long retirements, rushed to IRA headquarters in Dublin, only to find a bare cupboard. Determined to defend their people with the tactics of the past, these dissidents withdrew from the official Republican move-

---

[4] See J. Bowyer Bell, "The Escalation of Insurgency: The Provisional Irish Republican Army's Experience, 1969-1971," *Review of Politics,* vol. 35, no. 3 (July 1973), pp. 398-411.

ment to found the Provisional IRA. Known as the Provos, they sought to restore the old, "pure" rebel image. Although in 1969 and 1970, the first priority of the Provos was the defense of threatened Catholic areas, particularly in Derry and Belfast, the astute in the IRA recognized the existence of an opportunity to go over to the offensive. The British army, caught between Catholics and Protestants, increasingly favored the Protestant loyalists, who wanted to live under the Union Jack and to bring an end to change. By 1971 the Provos had provoked—though provocation was not always necessary—the British army into increasingly stringent repression. While this British response may have been tactically wise in the short run, it ultimately proved a strategic disaster by alienating the Catholics, paving the way for the IRA to transform itself into an aggressive revolutionary underground supported by much of the nationalist-Catholic population. At this point the new Conservative government in London, having long dithered and delayed in the face of rising violence, finally decided to introduce internment without trial throughout Ulster. As the Stormont regime knew when they advised the policy, this was not really a security measure, but rather another ritual humiliation of the Catholic minority. The internment policy, introduced in August 1971, proved brutal and ineffectual. Instead of crushing the IRA, the policy only further increased nationalist support for the new campaign against the British army. Thus internment provoked the very "terror" that all British efforts had in theory been fashioned to avoid.

By December 1971 the campaign had reached the point where the British home secretary admitted that the IRA could not be defeated, although there was hope that the violence could be reduced. Then in January 1972—on Bloody Sunday—British paratroopers shot and killed thirteen civilians during a civil-rights demonstration in Derry, further alienating the minority in the North and complicating the efforts of the Dublin government in the South to contain the IRA. In March, London imposed direct rule over Northern Ireland. The official IRA, fearful that more bombs would engender a civil war, announced a cease-fire. The Provos, however, kept up the bombing and sniping, determined not on mere concessions but on British withdrawal. Ultimately, in July, the Provo leaders succeeded in bombing their way to the bargaining table, meeting with the British minister for Irish affairs. When these talks collapsed, the British army moved into the IRA "no-go zones" and began a campaign of attrition that reduced the level of violence, but hardly to tolerable proportions.

During 1971 and 1972 the IRA—both the Provos and the officials of the regular IRA—concentrated their efforts on Northern Ireland itself and employed traditional urban and rural guerrilla tactics. Although the officials had bombed the Aldershot, England, regimental headquarters of the British paratroopers involved in the Bloody Sunday killings and there were one or two other independent forays, the troubles were confined to Ulster. The Provo IRA Council continued to see their operation as a military campaign in Ulster, and while they accepted that the British army could not be defeated with the Republican forces available, they believed that London could be persuaded to withdraw and let the Irish sort things out themselves. In the year following the adoption of internment, the Provos were riding high, with the number of their operations far surpassing the fabled record of the Tan War. Parts of Ulster became bombed and burnt war zones, with British armor on the streets and IRA gunmen around every corner. Those hotels which escaped destruction were filled with foreign journalists and television crews. Yet beyond Ireland these new troubles caused hardly a ripple. Even locally, the economic life of the province continued undisturbed. Compensation was paid for the bomb damage to commercial establishments, industry and the shipyards went untouched, and new British investment flowed in. The cost in pounds sterling to the British was relatively low. In fact, the troops shifted from NATO assignments cost less to maintain in Ulster than in Germany. Despite the Irish albatross, Britain could continue to contribute to NATO, and participate positively in the European community. If there was some sentiment in Britain for withdrawal, there was a more general consensus that the British should stick it out and save the Irish from themselves. By the end of 1972 the British presence had simply not yet cost enough in lives, in sterling, or in self-respect for London to give serious consideration to withdrawal.

By 1973 the Provos decided that an escalated bombing campaign would be more attractive than a continued war of attrition. British army pressure had begun to tell; the sympathetic nationalist population was war-weary. And at last London had initiated political changes that would create a new and fairer Northen Ireland Assembly. These changes put the Provos, militarily and politically, on the defensive. By 1974 the number of IRA "incidents" had declined. The Provo Army Council responded by authorizing a series of car bombings in London to be executed on the same day as the new Northern Ireland elections. Thus they hoped that the first step in the creation of a new "puppet" Ulster regime would be relegated to the second page of the newspapers and the British public would be made all too aware that the home island was not immune. The only visible results these "symbolic" bombings produced were the arrest, trial, and conviction of those involved, along with improved British security measures and general public indignation. There were several further waves of bombings, and although no one claimed responsibility, security forces assumed an Irish connection. The 1973–1975 bombings were ineffectual, apparently demonstrating typical Irish strategic incompetence and technical limitations. Neither a fire in Harrods nor the letter-bomb maiming of an Irish secretary in the British embassy in Washington was going to bring the Republic any closer, and the death of twenty-one innocents in a Birmingham pub alienated even Irish sympathizers.

Once Again, Failure. By 1975 the IRA campaign had become a spectacular and newsworthy display of terrorist violence, but in practical terms it has had little impact beyond the British Isles. Within a span of thirty years, the IRA had initiated an armed conflict three times—in 1939, 1956, and 1971—with varying local success, but each time with only minimal transnational impact. IRA activities during these years in Irish immigrant communities, particularly in the United States, caused some strains in Britain's international relations. And efforts to smuggle arms regularly attracted the attention of American law enforcement agencies in the 1970s, but there was nothing to equal the 1867 invasion of British Canada from American territory by an Irish force. IRA diplomatic contacts were never limited exclusively to Irish exiles, but except for the fumbling efforts to create a German connection between 1938 and 1941, threatening Irish neutrality, these have rarely engendered serious concern. Thus, as might be expected, there was considerable displeasure when London and Dublin discovered that the Provos were receiving arms from Libya given in the name of anti-imperialism and dismay in Washington when a version of the American M-16 rifle appeared in Ulster.

By and large, however, the IRA efforts to fuel the Ulster campaign produced a few spectacular failures and no serious international complications. The IRA factions had the capacity to spread the campaign beyond Great Britain, define new targets, and seek alternative roads.

But the leaders, acting within the Republican heritage and determined to wage a military campaign against the British army on Irish soil, cultivated their own revolutionary garden and failed to export violence. They authorized operations of symbolic terror in England only when momentum began to falter in 1973. Thus even Britain had remained largely immune to the Ulster troubles. And in 1975 the Provisional IRA announced a unilateral cease fire.

Summary. The first and most obvious conclusion to be drawn from the Irish experience is that Celtic rebels act within a tradition that endows their movement with legitimacy. They claim to act as reasonable men in the name of rational ideals.

The Irish Republicans assume that they act for the national ideal even when most of the Irish nation will not follow their lead, even when all the institutions of church and state deny them, and even as Irish prisons fill with Irish rebels. For them the Republican movement makes manifest the pure and unfaltering aspirations of Ireland. The distaste of the comfortable who hide behind constitutional barriers has no effect on rebels who contend that Irish institutions, spiritual or material, have long ago sold out the national ideals for the rewards of power. On such matters the rebel cares not for public opinion, for he "knows" that he represents the ideal and is the embodiment of that ideal. As De Valera once noted, he needed only to look into his own heart to know the desires of the Irish people. In Ireland, as elsewhere, those who wish to preserve law and order find this arrogant assumption of legitimacy, denied by the rebel to recognized institutions, a regular source of outrage. They object that the rebels' "mandate" often seems to permit the most ruthless and brutal acts, hiding violence under patriotic colors. Anyone who has seen the sheets of plate glass sent shattering into a crowded street by a car bomb is likely to reject any rebel rationale and doubt the existence of any rebel restraint. Yet the IRA campaign in Ulster operates within certain real bounds, avoiding certain violent variants popular elsewhere, and as a result, dreadful though they may be, IRA operations show a definite structure in contrast to the random, spontaneous vigilante campaign of the Ulster Protestants.

It is not that recourse to more widespread or transnational terror would harm the IRA image or is beyond its imagination or technical competence. The IRA simply has not seen the *need* to give up what it considers a "military" campaign, though many disinterested observers find their actions not much different than terrorism. In 1938, when the new IRA Council commanded a vastly eroded IRA, it had been unwilling to open a civil war in the South and fearful of sparking a Protestant pogrom in the North. In such a weak position, its only option had been to open a bombing campaign in Britain. The ineffectual campaign that followed can easily be described as transnational terror-bombing, because the rebel incompetence produced civilian casualties the IRA did not intend and because the technicality of operating across national boundaries made the bombings "international" in scope. In the fifties the ineffectual IRA guerrilla campaign scrupulously avoided the errors of the forties. This time the strategists felt that bombs were unnecessary and that such tactics would undermine the legitimacy of the struggle. In the 1970s the Provos no longer had any compunction about using bombs as a "military" technique for making Northern Ireland ungovernable, but only with grave reluctance did they authorize operations in Britain. Not until they faced loss of momentum and the growing effectiveness of British political initiatives did the Provo IRA feel the need to respond by widening the battleground.

Insurrection and Instability:
The African Experience

Despite the plethora of armed struggles which have shaken Africa during the last decade, there has been remarkably little recourse to techniques easily defined as transnational terrorism. African matters have remained largely African. The most visible of Africa's "forgotten" wars have been the armed struggles against the white bastions of South Africa, Rhodesia, and the Portuguese colonies, Angola and Mozambique in southern Africa and tiny Guinea-Bissau in West Africa. Approximately a dozen African national-liberation movements have for years sought power through revolutionary-guerrilla operations with varying success. South Africa and to some degree South-West Africa have largely resisted such operations. Elsewhere the rebels fought in the bush, unable to attack the cities and unwilling to resort to "terror." In Rhodesia a guerrilla campaign launched across the Zambezi River from Zambia collapsed by the end of the sixties after a series of blunders and catastrophic losses. In 1973 a renewed and more effective campaign against Rhodesia began when guerrillas, again based in Zambia, infiltrated through the bush country of Mozambique. In Mozambique, liberation movements were active for two years in the central province of Tete and in the north near the Tanzanian border, producing disorder but not much else. Three groups in Angola had much the same experience, while in West Africa the rebels in Guinea were somewhat more successful, restricting the Portuguese presence to fortified zones and the capital. During the colonial wars, the guerrillas forced the Portuguese to invest vast amounts in security operations; the percentage of Lisbon's total budget spent on military operations was among the highest in the world. Ultimately the Portuguese army rebelled, and the new regime opened negotiations with the African nationalists. It appeared that all the colonies would be independent by the end of 1975. Seeking an accommodation with Black Africa, South Africa began pressuring the settler regime in Rhodesia to open negotiations.

Without exception, all of these armed struggles remained within the narrow traditions of rural guerrilla practice. While the Rhodesians and Portuguese regularly called the Africans "terrorists," this was rarely a valid accusation. In fact, the two most spectacular transnational terrorist operations may have been organized by the Portuguese: the assassination in Senegal of Amilcar Cabral, leader of the PAIGC revolutionary group in Guinea-Bissau, and the assassination in Tanzania of Eduardo Mondlane, leader of the FRELIMO campaign in Mozambique. There were remarkably few operations in other countries or in Portugal and there was little urban activity. While most African nationalists, like their Latin American colleagues, held that they opposed the forces of "worldwide imperialism"—the colonial regimes were merely the immediate target—they made no attempt to wage the struggle against the distant Western imperialists. As a result, the African insurrections unfolded in relative isolation from Europe and America.

Of course, *any* insurrection except the most obscure and primitive does create a ripple effect through the transnational medium. A rebellion needs outside fuel and encouragement, and rebels always seek and need sanctuaries, training, and free movement in the outside world. The organization of such aid for those in rebellion against a government generally recognized as legitimate is bound to create transnational strains. Thus, for one purpose or another and at one time or another, a variety of non-African regimes have encouraged, if not sponsored, African liberation movements: North Korea, China, Russia, the Eastern European Communist bloc, and particularly Cuba. In Africa, the Organization of African Unity (OAU) created a Liberation Committee to coordinate regional aid to guerrillas. Liberation-front leaders regularly appear alongside conventional diplomatic delegates at African and international conferences. In a sense, the liberation movements became, and are recognized as, counterstates, forming an alternate and legitimate counterweight to the "immoral" or "outlaw" imperialist regimes. African revolutionary leaders are quite aware that this new "legitimacy" is a precious guerrilla asset and, consequently, have largely avoided any action that might harm their image of respectability.

Other guerrillas not so blessed must scramble for aid and comfort, and sometimes they resort to spectacular violence for want of other effective options. Since September 1961, the Eritrean Liberation Front (ELF) has been waging a guerrilla campaign in nothern Ethiopia with, until recently, only rare successes. Exploiting regional pride and dissident Muslim suspicion of the Christian center in Addis Ababa, the ELF had a further asset in the enthusiasm of many of the less sophisticated Eritreans, *shifta* eager for war and booty. To some degree there has always been an Eritrean bandit problem, for in the wilds these *shifta* have traditionally pursued a violent vocation for profit and out of pride. The *shifta*, many of them Muslims and suspicious of the Coptic Christian Empire, proved enthusiastic converts to guerrilla revolution and soon employed all the old bandit techniques under a new banner of national liberation. These techniques, however, led not to victory but to increasing Ethiopian repression so effective that at times it appeared that the Eritrean emergency had ended, that, at the most, only a bandit problem remained. Neither the Chinese aid, which gradually dwindled to a halt after Ethiopian Emperor Haile Selassie's visit to Peking, nor Libya's assistance to its fellow Muslims could effectively fuel the movement when the sophisticated leaders remained in exile and the *shifta* were largely left to their own devices. The result was that the truly dedicated turned to hijacking airliners, with mixed results. Thus a marginal and regional disorder that had only rarely caused any concern even in Addis Ababa and hardly ever anywhere else produced another quite real threat to international order. The ELF adopted a strategy of attacking aircraft, with attempted hijackings as far away as Madrid.[5]

---

[5] The Ethiopian response to hijacking was to take a very hard line indeed. Apparently, a considerable number of security people were aboard every flight with firm orders and considerable discretionary powers. Two ELF men who attempted a hijack over Madrid were captured and rushed to the first-class section, where they had their throats cut in a summary execution.

39

Once the Ethiopian army became deeply involved in a "coup on the installment plan" in 1974, the ELF regrouped, rearmed, and returned in force in 1975 to launch an almost open insurrection. "Terror" was no longer needed.

Even when African guerrillas eschew blatantly transnational tactics, as has been the case in the movements against the white African regimes, insurrectional disorder disturbs the world's normalcy: A bomb on the Benguela railway in Angola interrupted the flow of copper to the coast. A UN resolution on Guinea disturbed and embarrassed Western delegations. The arrival of Chinese AK-47s in Mozambique's Tete Province awakened new concerns about the export of revolution during a period of détente.

In any case, at least within an African context, the anti-imperialist struggle remains a popular cause. Among black Africans or Arabs there is no disagreement as to the necessity of pursuing the just struggle and the full need for sacrifice. Other African insurrections have placed far more severe strains on various regimes. For example, the long insurrection in the Southern Sudan which pitted not only North against South but also Islam against Christianity, English against Arabic, and black against brown produced real anxiety and strained loyalties in many African governments opposed to boundary changes which might open a pandora's box of separatist tribal demands all over Africa. The Ibo rebellion in Nigeria had much the same effect in certain quarters. And the Ethiopians found the concept of African unity difficult to adjust to the discovery that Libya was supporting the Eritrean rebels.

In the African experience with insurrection, overt terror has not been a favored option. Leaders of most African armed struggles have maintained a keen interest in shaping an appropriate image and seeking "legitimate"power. Thus, recourse to terror would be counterproductive. In the case of the ELF in Ethiopia, only when the *shifta* campaign faltered did the skyjacking begin. Though the transnational ripple-effect may resemble waves to those affected, the African insurrections have posed but a minor threat to world order. This may not always be so. Some movements may seek a release from constant frustration and failure and, acting on their professed ideological convictions, strike out against new imperialist targets. Some may appear in the cities—even in foreign cities—or some hidden militant core may feel impelled to begin a new campaign with a spectacular display. In Latin America, unlike Africa, the revolutionaries have been willing to adopt the tactics of terror, tactics that often have had international repercussions.

Latin American Revolutionaries:
The Tactics of Terror in Revolutionary Strategies

In Latin America political violence often appears endemic, an institutionalized and endless cycle of disorder. The tradition of disruption is historically well established. Before 1912 there were fifty-two important revolts in Venezuela, and in subsequent years the rule of military leaders was repeatedly challenged. During the nineteenth century there were some sixty revolts in Bolivia, in Haiti a succession of assassinated presidents, in Colombia repeated civil wars, and everywhere a dreary round of coups and *caudillos*. In the twentieth century the success of Latin American revolutionary movements has been mixed. The Mexican revolution brought limited and institutionalized change; the Bolivian revolution, on the heels of the electoral victory of the Nationalist Revolutionary Movement in 1952, produced not a new order, but twenty years of violent challenge to the reforms. The Cuban revolution of Fidel Castro, under Russian aegis, did bring a new order to that country, but elsewhere in Latin America little changed or little change was attempted. Despite promises and apparent sincerity, one elite group or dominant personality followed another, often violently, with little effect upon the established order. In Colombia, after months of violence following the April 1948 assassination of liberal leader Jorge Eliécer Gaitán, the country slipped into more than a decade of violence that may have taken over 200,000 lives and that saw the greatest rural armed mobilization in Latin America since the Mexican Revolution. In the 1960s alone there were seventeen successful military coups, several more near misses, and a great many plots that aborted in the planning. Although the revolutionaries contributed their share to the level of violence, with the exception of Cuba they did so without the reward of gained power. Only Chile and Uruguay have (most of the time) stood outside this pattern of violent disorder.

Distant and often uninformed observers of Latin America tend to equate violence with revolutionary politics in Latin America, yet often the region's violence has other sources. Rafael Trujillo made the Dominican Republic his personal fiefdom from 1931 to 1961 by means of institutional authorized terror, as did François Duvalier in Haiti between 1957 and 1971.

41

Contemporary Latin American revolutionary history began on 2 December 1956, when eighty-two insurgents led by Fidel Castro landed on a Cuban beach. What happened between the initial contact with the Cuban army that reduced rebel strength to twelve and the glorious—and so far unique—moment when the *barbudos* came down out of the hills and took power in Havana on 1 January 1959 has since dominated all revolutionary considerations. There has been, of course, little agreement on what really happened or what strategic lessons can be learned from the Cuban experience. For a decade and a half Latin American revolutionaries have derived theories from the Cuban effort only to find these inapplicable to their own struggles.

The revolutionaries first decided that the major problem was the initial seizure of power, for after this had been accomplished the United States would not intervene and Russia might protect the new regime. This lesson was reconsidered after the Bay of Pigs fiasco in 1961, challenged during the missile crisis of October 1962, and rejected after the American intervention in the Dominican Republic in 1965. By then a generation had accepted the principle that a revolution would require geographically widespread success so that the new rebel regimes could not be isolated. Douglas Bravo, one of the leaders of the new wave in Venezuela, produced a thesis that reflected the internationalism of all his Latin American guerrilla colleagues:

> The Venezuelan revolution is part of a chain of national liberation movements which, throughout the world, are struggling to be rid of imperialist domination. To be more concrete, the Venezuelan revolution is an integral part of the movement for Latin American independence. It is impossible to remove any one Latin American national revolution from the contest of the struggle of the peoples of Latin America against North American imperialism.
>
> The revolution is clearly continental in character, even though it has certain specific features of its own, and the path chosen is determined both by these specific features and by the general context of Latin American republics.[6]

Thus the big picture was clear; the enemy was North American imperialism, represented locally by oppressive puppet regimes. The struggle was to be international in scope but regionally specific in technique.

[6] Luis Mercier Vega, *Guerrillas in Latin America: The Technique of the Counterstate* (New York: Praeger, 1969), p. 219.

Determining these specifics of revolutionary strategy and tactics proved very complicated. The immediate revolutionary response to Castro's victory was to copy his method exactly. On 18 April 1959, an expedition mimicking the Castro descent on Cuba landed in Panama and was scooped up within a few hours. A similar effort beginning on 28 May of the samè year in Nicaragua collapsed in a few months. Two weeks later two landings were made in the Dominican Republic and the rebels were wiped out within a few hours. A 14 August landing in Haiti failed within days. Clearly, more care and preparation were necessary, but the consensus remained that the Cuban experience would prove fruitful for others. Out of the years 1956–1958, Che Guevara had parsed three principals:

1. The people's forces can win a war against the regular army;
2. It is not necessary to wait until all conditions are favorable to start a revolution; the insurrection itself can bring about those conditions;
3. In the underdeveloped nations of America, the basic field of action for armed struggle must be the countryside.[7]

Once the stage of improvised expeditions had passed, more serious consideration was given to the careful injection of guerrilla *foci*—mother cells of revolution—into rural areas, following again the Cuban experience as detailed by Guevara. Attempts along these lines failed in central Peru in 1962, in northern Argentina in 1963–1964, in southern Brazil in 1964, and again in central Peru in 1965. Guevara's own attempt failed in Bolivia in 1967, as did a subsequent effort in northern Argentina the next year. Few of the revolutionary *foci* lasted more than a few months once they came to the notice of security forces. Nowhere had there been adequate local preparation. Nowhere did the cherished peasant population convert to the revolutionary cause as a result of the armed struggle. Certainly the pure *foco* theory, elaborated by Régis Debray in *Revolution in the Revolution,* appeared little more than a romantic, if tempting, misreading of the Cuban experience, an experience that demonstrably must have been more complex than Guevara and the others assumed. Long before Guevara arrived in the Bolivian *altiplano*, other Latin Americans had discovered firsthand the rocks on the revolutionary road that somehow Castro had evaded and Guevara

---

[7] Che Guevara, *Guerrilla Warfare* (New York: Monthly Review Press, 1961), p. 15.

had ignored, and no place in the years immediately after the Cuban triumph had the road to revolution appeared as promising as in Venezuela.

Venezuela: The Frustration of Revolution. In November 1948 a military coup led by Pérez Jiménez overthrew the three-year-old regime of Rómulo Betancourt, leader of the *Acción Democrática* and one of Latin America's best known liberals. The leaders of the fallen government went into exile. Pérez Jiménez, unappealing in both person and habits, ruled as *caudillos* were wont to do, with arrogance and greed and without much effort to fashion a benevolent image. In time the plight of the poor and the gross incompetence and corruption of the government alienated even the conservatives and the Church. To buttress his position, Pérez Jiménez manipulated a plebiscite in December 1957 that produced an overwhelming "vote of confidence" but a further decay of support. On 1 January 1958, a revolt at the air base at Maracay was successfully suppressed, but Pérez Jiménez felt pressured to dismiss his more unsavory colleagues. His action was too late. On 14 January rioting began in Caracas. On 21 January a general strike coupled with street fighting forced Jiménez to accept reality, and on 23 January he flew to exile in the Dominican Republic. Rear Admiral Wolfgang Larrazabal took over, added civilian cabinet ministers, and on 27 January promised elections within the year. The exiles returned and Venezuela settled in to a year of conventional political maneuvering.

The old political leaders, in particular those who had been in Betancourt's *Acción Democrática,* found on their return that a new generation determined on radical change had arisen. Throughout the political establishment there was a visible split between the exiles and those who had remained, between the young and the old, tired and optimistic, radical and reluctant. Still, with an effective party organization Betancourt won the December 1958 elections, drawing just under 50 percent of the vote in a three-man race that saw a 93 percent turnout. Many throughout Latin America sensed a heartening trend away from the decade of despots. The Venezuelan radicals, however, had their doubts. The new president, while maintaining his liberal image abroad, soon revealed himself to be anti-Communist, anti-Castro, and anti-revolutionary. Perhaps no one could have transformed the dreams of the Venezuelan militants into reality. For them the 1958 "revolution" had apparently ended with the presidential elections.

In August 1959 guards fired on a demonstration of the unemployed in Caracas. Peasant efforts to seize land were rebuffed. Student protests were crushed. By the end of the year, the radicals were convinced that Betancourt had sold out to the conservatives and the Americans. In April 1960 the radical wing of *Acción Democrática* split off, taking fourteen of the seventy-three *Acción* legislative deputies and much of the youth wing into the new *Movimiento de Izquierda Revolucionaria* (MIR). The 20 October 1960 arrest of six MIR members for subversion began a cycle of protest demonstrations and police repressions that led to six deaths by the end of the month. Although the leadership of the MIR had organized as a "constitutional alternative," the continued rigor of the repression during November and December nudged the party toward revolution. By the end of the year, it had become clearer that protest in the streets would spark not an insurrection, as some in the MIR had assumed, but only military repression. Yet Betancourt appeared increasingly vulnerable. A further twenty-six deputies had broken with *Acción Democrática.* Even the usually cautious Venezuelan Communist party appeared to be drifting toward a revolutionary commitment. And always there was the example of Castro and the *barbudos,* the victorious revolutionaries who were transforming Cuba.

During 1960–1961, the Venezuelan radicals discarded first the coalition politics and *Acción Democrática,* then the original constitutional strategy of the MIR, and finally hopes for a popular insurrection in Caracas. In 1962 even the Communists accepted the presence of a mature revolutionary situation and the need for an armed struggle, this time based on rural guerrilla combat. (The switch to the country and away from urban demonstrations and riots arose from practical necessity and was not an application of the Cuban experience.) In any case, the results left much to be desired. MIR-Communist guerrilla groups were scattered over much of the country. Quickly organized and loosely controlled, their haphazard efforts reflected a lack of proper arms and training and an enthusiasm that often waned under pressure.

Beginning in January, the Venezuelan military reacted vigorously to the guerrilla challenge. Many of the groups were scattered or destroyed and the leaders killed or captured. The surviving units fell out of contact. There was seldom any direction from Caracas and often little cooperation between the various revolutionary sponsors. Two unsuccessful military risings did bring some leftist officers into the guerrilla movements and further weakened Betancourt. However, nothing could disguise the

45

fact that 1962 had not been a vintage year for Venezuelan revolution. The urban cadres had been mauled, the rural guerrillas badly defeated, and Betancourt, if increasingly unpopular, had weathered challenges from both left and right.

Still, there was no option for the rebels but to go on, hopefully with more coherence. On 20 February 1963, the revolutionary allies, the Communists, the MIR, radical idealists, and the disgruntled officers-turned-guerrillas set up the *Fuerzas Armadas de Liberación Nacional* (FALN) and a Communist-sponsored *Frente de Liberación Nacional* (FLN), which was responsible for political decisions. By then there was evidence that the Venezuelan revolutionary strategy had entered a new phase, again in part determined by the lack of other options.

On 27 October 1962 the power stations of the American Creole Petroleum Company had been attacked. In November American oil company pipelines had been sabotaged. There had been demonstrations against "North American imperialism" before 1962, most notably the riot around Vice President Richard Nixon's limousine in May 1958, but the FALN now intended to broaden the armed struggle. In February 1963 the Sears and Roebuck warehouse in Caracas was burned, as was the United States Military Mission in June. Increasingly, this new generation of revolutionaries, emboldened by events in Cuba and Vietnam, admirers of Ho Chi Minh and Che Guevara, and determined internationalists, would see North American targets, official or private, as legitimate—symbols or implements of covert Yankee imperialism.

More spectacular were the urban operations that foreshadowed a new revolutionary decade of guerrilla warfare far from bush and jungle. One set of tactics, known as the "Robin Hood option," garnered publicity, amused the public, and embarrassed the regime. On 16 January 1963 the FALN raided an exhibition of French paintings, carrying off works by Cezanne, Van Gogh, Gauguin, Braque, and Picasso. All were returned three days later. On 11 February, the cargo ship *Anzoategue* was seized by armed stowaways and, after sending various FALN revolutionary radio messages, sailed into Brazilian waters. On 24 August an Argentine football star was kidnapped by FALN "policemen" and released two days later, reportedly bewildered by Venezuelan politics. The deputy chief of the United States Military Mission was kidnapped, only to be released eight days later with shoe polish in his hair. The very next day, FALN members hijacked an airliner, dropped leaflets, and forced the pilot to fly to Trinidad. When authorities there refused

46

to give the rebels asylum, returning them to Venezuela, the FALN organized retaliatory machine-gun attacks on the embassies of Trinidad and Great Britain. Such revolutionary stunts did not comprise the central thrust of the FALN's new urban offensive because guerrilla reality was hardly amusing in the cities.

Beginning in the last months of 1962 and lasting until early 1964, particularly during the spring and summer of 1963, there was virtually constant gunfire in Caracas. The FALN conducted a campaign to kill at least one policeman each day, and did so for 500 straight days. At night firing was often continuous. Buildings were seized and briefly held and government patrols were ambushed by snipers firing from windows and disappearing. On 12 June 1963 an attempt to assassinate President Betancourt in Ciudad Bolivar barely failed. Urban tactical groups robbed banks, seized radio stations to broadcast appeals, and took over movie theaters and gave lectures. With a strategic mix of the spectacular and the lethal, the FALN sought to destroy civil order and then, with the aid of the revitalized rural guerrilla columns, sweep into power. To some observers such aspirations did not seem unreasonable.

In response the regime determined to continue with the presidential elections scheduled for December 1963 and to continue to allow the police rather than the military to bear the main burden in Caracas. It also decided to suppress the still-legal radical organizations. In October 1963, Communist and MIR deputies and leaders were arrested. Partially in response to the arrests, but also in further hopes of disrupting the elections, the FALN called a general strike in November that produced two days of rioting and twenty deaths in Caracas before finally petering out.

On 1 December, the FALN was dealt what in time would prove a fatal blow; 90 percent of the electorate went to the polls and elected *Acción Democrática* candidate Raul Leoni president. The FALN boycott was a total failure, and worse, Betancourt, the ideal enemy who had alienated everyone and destroyed his own party, had left the scene. As Douglas Bravo, one of the most determined FALN leaders, noted, "It must be admitted that the triumph of *Acción Democrática,* supported by the oligarchy and imperialism, was the first great defeat of the popular movement." [8] Perhaps, as Moses Moliere of the MIR suggested, the government had won only "a skirmish in the long battle for national

---

[8] Richard Gott, *Guerrilla Movements in Latin America* (London: Nelson, 1970), p. 131.

liberation," [9] but a decade later that battle would show no signs of producing a satisfactory conclusion for the revolutionaries. In 1964 many of the old militants began to withdraw as the Communists drew back and the dedicated became fewer. The struggle in the cities sputtered and ended. The only option for the faithful was to resort again to rural guerrilla war, a choice that could guarantee survival but not victory: "Guerrilla units may survive without help from the towns, but they cannot develop without it." [10] Another decade has passed, and the Venezuelan revolutionaries have still found no effective way to return to the towns.

The various strategic options fashioned by the Venezuelan revolutionaries had largely been imposed by events rather than adopted for theoretical reasons. There had been little time to consider alternatives or to analyze the rushing events properly. The MIR had been created because the radicals discovered that Betancourt had become an unsatisfactory vehicle for their aspirations, but how those aspirations, often unarticulated, could be satisfied by "constitutional" means no one knew. Faced with repression in the cities, the rebels by necessity initiated a rural guerrilla campaign, but this was ill-organized and without central direction. Failing once again, the FALN returned to the city, but this time, eschewing demonstrations, it instead adopted a variety of the ingenious and ruthless tactics of urban guerrillas. Over the next decade the Venezuelan experience would be repeated, whether by design or not, under various conditions and for differing purposes by other revolutionaries seeking a swift path to power.

Strategies of Revolution. Increasingly, throughout Latin America it became clear what it was that prompted so many revolutionaries to follow —often unknowingly and always with equal frustration—the Venezuelan experience. First, as had been the case in Venezuela, electoral politics seldom satisfied those avid for vast and immediate change. And revolution by election, already discredited, lost its last advocates after the 1973 Chilean coup. Thus, if as seemed necessary, there was to be an armed struggle, there appeared to be several obvious options: (1) an insurrectionary rising, (2) a largely rural guerrilla campaign, either with extensive central organization or sparked by *foci,* (3) a largely urban guerrilla campaign, or (4) a mix of all three of these. Few continued

---

[9] Ibid.
[10] Ibid., p. 165.

to have great hopes for mass risings, for repeatedly loyal government forces had reacted to such challenges with rigor, and often the revolutionary cadres found themselves alone at the barricade. The two rural options continued to attract converts, even after Guevara's death in 1967 and even after the failure of any of the rural columns to pose a serious threat to the system. The pure *foco* concept, however, passed away with its creator, Guevara. There had been great hopes for the urban option, for if the Venezuelan effort had been largely undermined by election results, this would hardly be the case for a Latin America mostly dominated by dictators. The new theorists assumed that once begun, a spectacular urban campaign could be escalated and expanded.

The perhaps most influential of these, Carlos Marighella, who in his fifties had resigned from the Communist party of Brazil to lead the armed struggle, believed that the great need was to begin immediately and so initiate the effort in the cities:

> In 1968 we weren't yet a national organization. We were only a revolutionary group in São Paulo with almost no resources, and our ties to the rest of the country were almost nonexistent. . . . We grew as a result of action, only and exclusively as a result of revolutionary action. . . . We began urban guerrilla warfare in fact, but without publicly saying so . . . our enemies were caught by surprise. . . . The concrete manifestations of the revolutionary was surged forth in the large cities in Brazil in 1968 through urban guerrilla warfare and psychological warfare—forerunners of the rural guerrillas in our country.[11]

The rural guerrillas Marighella hoped for never came. Instead there was only vigorous repression, counter-terror, and murder by vigilantes. On 4 November 1969 Brazilian police shot and killed Marighella. Within a year most of the urban guerrillas were dead, jailed, or exiled. Another round of terrorist efforts had aborted. The theorists noted that just as in the country, a revolutionary *foco* could begin in the city, but, if isolated, would also end there. The key was the appropriate mix of strategies and the choice of the ideal moment for initiating the attack.

Such a moment continually escaped the revolutionaries in Latin America. Even where conditions appeared most ripe and the strategy ideal, the results were disastrous. In Guatemala, a country dominated by a small, arrogant, often corrupt elite, the rebels could not devise the

---

[11] Carlos Marighella, *Mini-Manual of Guerrilla Warfare* (Havana: Tricontinental, January 1970), pp. 54-56.

proper urban-rural mix. Despite spectacular operations and despite a very high level of violence—perhaps ten thousand people were killed—they could never force the collapse of the center. In Uruguay the problem was different; there was no room for a rural guerrilla campaign nor any need for one, since half the population lived in the capital. The elaboration of the old spectacular urban tactics by the Tupamaros produced extensive press coverage and attracted the avid interest of still another revolutionary generation, but, as elsewhere, led only to repression and despair, if not total defeat. By the end of the decade following the FALN's return to the cities in 1962, all Latin American revolutionary strategies had failed in their practical application, no matter what the mix of tactics. Yet, given their refusal to resign themselves to continued oppression and abandon the people, the revolutionaries, unlike the Latin American middle-class liberals, have been unwilling to seek change through conventional political means, and unlike the Communists, not willing to wait for mature revolutionary conditions. They *had* to find a means to act on events. Increasingly, the tactics of urban violence have become not the means to gain power itself, but rather an effort to take some effective action in order to maintain organization and hope until the long-sought mature revolutionary situation might appear. The rebels, after a decade of buffeting, still felt that to give up the armed struggle for any merely political action—even the crucial organization of the masses—would mean to give up any hope of revolution for their generation. And so resigning themselves to the fact that they could not become a counter-state in the seventies, they sought to create with the tactics of the urban guerrilla a countervailing force to influence events they could not control.

Argentina: The Persistence of Revolution. Despite an economic potential almost unequalled in Latin America, Argentina has never found a formula that would produce continuing prosperity combined with political stability. Juan Perón's remarkable attempt to base the future of the country on the poor, particularly the urban poor, foundered because of conservative resistance and his own errors. Although Perón went into exile in 1955, he left a legacy of popularism that with the passage of years grew more attractive to those who had become alienated by a series of less than charismatic leaders who were apparently without administrative talent or vision and certainly without luck. After 1966 a series of military regimes mismanaged the economy, suppressed any opposition, and alienated even the conservatives. Investment was down; the economy sluggish, and traditionally high grain and beef exports declined, as, consequently, did foreign currency reserves. Unemployment climbed in a stagnating economy. There was little foreign investment and no answer to inflation. General Alejandro Agustin Lanusse, who had taken over in a coup in April 1970, found more problems than prestige in his presidency. In 1971 he opened discussions with moderate party leaders concerning a return to elected, constitutional government to replace the palace generals who had been in power since 1966.

Considerably before Lanusse's change of heart, others in Argentina had sought more direct means to transform the country. Almost since Perón's departure in 1955, there had been organized secret underground groups dedicated to his return. The most stable was the *Fuerzas Armadas Perónistas* (FAP), which represented the Perónist left and absorbed the more radical militants. In July 1971 three extreme Peronist groups merged with the FAP, and contacts with other revolutionary groups produced a guerrilla alliance. The *"Juan Jose Valle" Montoneros* Perónists appeared in June 1970 and found the link with the FAP congenial. The third partner was the *Fuerzas Armadas Revolucionarias* (FAR), representing the internationalist trend in revolutionary strategy engendered by Che. The FAR had, in fact, been organized in 1966 and 1967 to cooperate in the grand *foco altiplano* strategy that had come to grief with the failure of Che's Bolivian *foco*. FAR cadres found little difference between aspirations of the other Peronist guerrillas and their own. All three groups abhored the military and police, opposed multinational corporations—particularly those of North America—and admired Castro's successes. An equally violent, if more ideologically narrow, guerrilla group, *Ejército Revolucionario del Pueblo* (ERP), had come into being in May 1969 as a military wing of the *Partido Revolucionario de Trabajadores,* the banned Trotskyites. While all the guerrilla groups had before them the revolutionary experience of the decade, in 1970 and 1971 the prospects of an urban campaign still offered promise, given the then remarkable and spectacular success of the Tupamaros across the Rio de la Plata in Montevideo. Most important, the Perónist movement had survived as a mass movement for fifteen years despite official repression, and the elderly Perón in his Spanish exile remained a useful if distant idol. Thus, unlike the Tupamaros, the FALN, or Marighella, the Perónist guerrillas could act within a broad political front instead of as an isolated revolutionary

51

group with few resources. Consequently, 1970 and 1971 saw intensive guerrilla activity, as old groups like the Castroite *Fuerzas Armadas de Liberación* dropped by the wayside and new ones like the ERP appeared.

The tactics of the loosely structured Perónist guerrilla alliance mirrored those employed elsewhere in Latin America, with an added dash of ruthlessness. Between January 1969 and July 1971, fifty-three Argentine police were killed by guerrillas. In May 1970, former President Aramburu was kidnapped and killed by the *Montoneros.* The ERP kidnapped a British consul and the FAP assassinated a former chief of police. Guerrillas raided banks, shot isolated soldiers, attacked police stations, seized radio stations, and raided armories. By mid-1971 the government estimated that Argentina contained 6,000 subversives. The response of the regime had been typical in its repressive tactics. They were, however, applied in a unique strategic context; for in March 1972, Lanusse extended political negotiation and discussion to include Perónists, and, some believe, Perón himself. Thus he undermined the Perónist guerrilla complaints about an electoral farce that would undoubtedly return worn-out politicians. Subsequent guerrilla action would have to be justified in terms of Perónist politics, not simply as opposition to the military regime. In any case, from his Spanish exile Perón had given his blessings to the guerrillas: "If I were fifty years younger I would understandably go about planting bombs or meting out my own brand of justice." [12] Of course, Perón's policies did not limit the ERP or the other non-Perónist groups, but the prospects of a real election should have changed the context of the guerrilla campaign. In fact, there was little evidence of any change toward moderation, for August saw one of the more spectacular guerrilla operations. The ERP, the FAR, and the *Montoneros* guerrillas freed a group of prisoners at Trelew in southern Argentina, while another group seized the airstrip there and hijacked an airliner. Six of the escaped prisoners, including Mario Roberto Santucho, head of the ERP, flew on to Chile before Argentine security forces closed in on the Trelew airstrip. Nineteen of the guerrillas were captured and ten escaped. Obviously, the military regime's prestige had been badly damaged. Six days later, sixteen prisoners in Trelew, including Santucho's pregnant wife, were killed "while trying to escape." The nearly universal condemnation of the regime for this act did little to restore stability or to persuade the guerrillas to moderation.

---

[12] *New York Times*, 24 January 1974.

During the electoral campaign, which was open to Perónist candidates but not Perón himself, there was little reduction in the level of violence, particularly on the part of the ERP. While the Perónist guerrillas regarded the elections with mixed emotions, this was not so for the ERP:

> The People's Revolutionary Army firmly believes that the definitive road to national and social liberation will not be realized through elections. Power is not born from votes. Power is born from gunpoint. While these are in the hands of repressive forces and not in the hands of the people, the generals and exploiters of the country will continue in power.[13]

Three days later the Perónist candidate won the election. Perón's own choice for president, Hector J. Campora, who had already promised the guerrilla prisoners amnesty, was to take power on 25 May 1973. In the meantime, since the guns were still not in the hands of the people, ERP guerrillas remained active. An army intelligence officer was assassinated; an Argentine manager of an American bank was kidnapped; an executive of Kodak and a retired admiral were kidnapped on the same day; and later in April, a former army chief of staff was assassinated by the ERP. Apparently, ERP leaders believed that such actions would persuade the Perónist movement to break with the military, or failing that, provoke the military into a repression that would engender a real revolution. In any case, the ERP announced that it would take a watchdog role over events. The Perónists sought to calm the military, their own militant supporters, and the other guerrillas. The continuing violence not only built up pressures within the military establishment to intervene, but also began to erode the broad Perónist front. The ERP would not be reassured and announced that operations would continue unless the new government adopted a revolutionary course.

Campora took office, waited fifty days, and then resigned so that a September election could return Perón himself to power. These two months saw an acceleration of violence, including a series of assassinations within the Perónist labor movement. During a press conference in June, ERP leaders announced that they would not attack the Perónist regime itself if it did not repress the people, but that operations would continue against the armed forces, counter-revolutionaries, foreign exploiters, and Argentine capitalists. By early August there had been over 100 kidnappings and a growing series of open attacks on "reac-

---

[13] *New York Times*, 9 March 1973.

53

tionary" targets by militant leftists within a Perónist movement which was increasingly becoming seriously divided.

The interim Perónist government finally announced that it would put an end to destructive action by minority groups. Toleration of the guerrillas had ended. In September Perón was elected as expected, and as predicted he began to purge the movement of the militant leftists. The assassinations continued, as did the other operations of the guerrillas. American companies were bombed and foreign executives were kidnapped. The most profitable incident proved to be the ERP kidnapping on 6 December 1973 of Victor Samuelson, an Exxon Corporation executive, that resulted in a record $14.2 million ransom, ultimately paid in March 1974 without even the immediate release of the hostage. There is no accurate count of incidents or operations, but in Buenos Aires alone over 400 guerrillas were killed by security forces. Though the situation was chaotic, Perón was in place. The militant left in his movement had been excluded and the military apparently was content that there would be no more concessions to the guerrillas. On 25 January 1974, eight months after repealing the old military regime's anti-terrorist legislation, the Argentine Congress passed a stringent new anti-terrorist bill that doubled many prison sentences and transferred internal-security functions to the federal police. Perón noted that the "small number of psychopaths who are still left will be exterminated one by one for the good of the republic." [14] Meanwhile, the "psychopaths" continued their onslaught of terror. By the end of the year the regime was still under seige. Perón had died, and his wife, who succeeded him as president, was no more successful in ending the violence. Late in December the assassin's toll for the year had passed 220. In 1975 the assassinations, guerrilla raids and kidnappings continued. By September more than 500 people had been killed. The *Montoneros* had reputedly been paid a $60 million ransom for two industrialists. A right-wing guerrilla group appeared. The economy was in chaos and Isabel Perón "on vacation."

Summary. Until the Lanusse opening to the Perónists, the various Argentine guerrilla groups were typical of the current wave of urban revolutionary militants attacking Latin American governments and North American and other "imperialist" targets as a first stage in a campaign that they hoped would expand. Once the orthodox Perónists

---

[14] *New York Times*, 26 January 1974.

entered electoral politics, the Perónist guerrillas saw their actions as a means to pressure the moderates to keep the revolutionary faith. With Campora's election, the campaign increasingly became an effort of the various "watch-dog" guerrillas to coerce the Perónist establishment into a revolutionary policy by hitting targets that included even conservative Perónists.

That a group like the ERP could anticipate waging guerrilla war against the same old targets without the interference of the new regime was some indication of the tortuous logic of men who refused any compromise. As a coercive and violent pressure group, they might have had a case before Campora, but continuing the same behavior under a Perónist regime simply polarized the country asymmetrically, isolating the militant left and alienating Perón, who was now more conservative in any case. The guerrillas had to return to an urban strategy based on a tiny following opposed to the popular sentiment demonstrated in the electoral results. And this came at the very time that the Tupamaros in Uruguay were being badly shaken by similar errors.

The very tactical success of the Argentine guerrilla groups in 1972 and 1973, which might have led to substantial results, had clouded the guerrillas' vision. Total victory had never been possible, but violence might have produced gains if it had been employed in moderation, if the "Robin Hood option" had been chosen instead of the way of the assassin. Thus a most interesting potential guerrilla strategy—with the guerrilla as a violent pressure group, an armed watchdog—collapsed back into the previous stage of urban warfare with a limited political base comprised only of the extreme left. No doubt the Argentine militants can continue to engender chaos, as did other Latin American movements in either an early stage or after the main momentum had been lost, but the chance to effect change seems to have passed.

The Latin American experience indicates that revolutionary recourse to the tactics of terror, particularly in an urban campaign, can have distressing effects on civic order without necessarily achieving guerrilla ends. The most effective operations have often been the least violent. Kidnapping a foreign executive for a ransom to be given to the poor may not be popular with Ford or Firestone, but may be favorably viewed by the local population. Because such tactics as kidnapping or attacks against multinational companies are both popular and profitable, there is little doubt that such means will become conventional in future campaigns. The murder of imperialist diplomats and foreign executives, on the other hand, has had mixed results, no matter what the rationalizations of the guerrillas. The Latin American rebels have devised and employed a most impressive collection of tactical maneuvers, but have yet to find an effective long-range strategy. At best such tactics can maintain the movement until an effective strategy can be devised. In the Middle East, however, the tactics of terror have been elaborated into a comprehensive terrorist strategy.

The Palestinian Fedayeen: The Strategy of Terror

False Dawn. At the beginning of June 1967, everything at last seemed possible for the Arabs. Euphoric crowds under huge black banners rushed through the streets of Cairo. Everywhere radio stations broadcast predictions of imminent triumph over the Zionists. Even the skeptics in cosmopolitan Lebanon appeared moved by the possibilities. It appeared as if, by a fantastic series of cunning maneuvers, the central hero of the Arab drama, Gamal Abdul Nasser of Egypt, was about to transform history, erase the old humiliations, and achieve the Arabs' long-denied dream of victory over their most adamant foe, the Zionists of Israel. By the end of June, after one of the most crushing defeats in modern military history, the situation seemed more hopeless than ever. Vengeance had become an idle dream. And within the Arab world none had fallen as far from the heady days of early June as the Palestinians, victims once again of Arab incompetence. Seemingly, in every decade since the arrival of the Zionists, the position of the Palestinian Arabs had decayed until they had become a people cursed, prisoners in their own land or scattered in mean exile. Betrayed, denied, and dependent upon charity, there appeared no hope for them after the combined military power of the Arab states had been so completely destroyed in the Six-Day War.

The Rise of the PLO. During that bleak summer of 1967, hope was unexpectedly offered by an organization that previously played a miniscule role in the Middle East confrontation, the tiny Palestine Liberation Movement, al Fatah, which was dedicated to guerrilla revolution. Like many other radical Arab movements, al Fatah had emerged before the 1967 war, feeding on the dreams of young men frustrated with the leadership of their elders, with the conventional wisdom, and with the evil tolerated by the comfortable. The militants of al Fatah felt that the Palestinians themselves, through a guerrilla revolution fought by "commandos," or fedayeen, could triumph over Zionism. They believed that there no longer need be a resigned Palestinian dependence on the conventional armies of conventional Arab states.

Realizing that some place, some how, someone must strike the first blow, al Fatah, with eighty-two men, had begun the armed struggle against Israel on 1 January 1965. Escalation had been halting; from January to June 1967, the fedayeen had succeeded in killing fourteen Israelis, wounding 72, and carrying out 122 acts of sabotage. The June War had completely overshadowed the fedayeen, who were largely as optimistic at the beginning of June as other Arabs. At that point, they had to watch rather than shape events. After the war, however, the fedayeen offered a coherent strategy of revolution, which promised ultimate triumph not only because the cause was just, but also, it was argued, because the way of the revolutionary guerrilla must inevitably prove effective. Fedayeen leaders noted the fertile ground for revolt in the Israeli-occupied zones of Gaza and the West Bank. Increasingly the young, shamed by June's events, the displaced who had fled into deeper exile, and those attracted to the luminous vision of guerrilla warfare flooded into al Fatah. The radicals who had previously insisted on a world revolution or at least a pan-Arab revolution—who had offered the way of the Baathist or of Nasserism or of communism— found themselves sudden converts to a guerrilla revolution focused on Palestine. Fedayeen organizations sprang up throughout the Middle East, representing every political current and posture and sometimes surviving only through charisma or the resources of an individual leader.

In the confusion of schisms and splinter groups, al Fatah retained a central position. It was the first and the largest of the Palestinian groups on the scene and was uncommitted to a narrow ideological position. Thus the organization tended to represent a fedayeen con- sensus. Al Fatah saw Israel as an artificial state inserted within the Middle East for Western purposes, a state which would prove vulnerable to guerrilla revolution. After a fedayeen victory had been accomplished, al Fatah argued, the Jews would discard their false Zionist ideals and take their place in a secular, binational, and democratic Palestine. And the fedayeen increasingly believed they were fashioning the means to that end through a guerrilla strategy that seemed to bring triumph closer each month. Soon there was not just hope but certainty:

> Israel is undoubtedly engaged in a losing battle, as the forces
> of the Palestine liberation movement acquire experience and

achieve the strategic depth provided by the Palestinian and Arab masses. However long it takes, their struggle represents another historical example of a people's inevitable triumph over colonialism, racism, and oppression.[15]

And even if the struggle did take somewhat longer than anticipated, it would transform the humiliated Palestinians, creating in the cauldron of battle a renewed people:

> Violence will purify the individuals from venom, it will redeem the colonized from inferiority complex, it will return courage to the countryman.
> Blazing our armed revolution inside the occupied territory is a healing medicine for all our people's diseases.[16]

By 1968 the Palestinian fedayeen had become a considerable phenomenon. Charming and articulate, eager fedayeen spokesmen related in detail repeated victories on the battlefield, ran guided tours of the guerrilla camps, and generated a heady atmosphere of action. The quarrels and wrangles within the Palestinian movement that produced a dozen splinter groups were ignored, and the constant interference by various interested Arab regimes was played down. Within the Arab world, criticism of the fedayeen became cautious after efforts to restrict guerrilla activities in Lebanon and Jordan sparked riots.

In March 1968, an Israeli retaliation raid on the fedayeen base at Karameh in Jordan ran into heavy resistance. The base was destroyed; 200 fedayeen were killed and 128 were taken prisoner; but there were also heavy Israeli losses, mostly accounted for by Jordanian army artillery fire. Many Arabs, thinking only of the fedayeen involvement, transformed Karameh into a guerrilla victory. Yet, to the careful observer it began to appear that a great many of the fedayeen's "victories" were largely the reflection of wish fulfillment. The guerrillas had not been able to fashion an effective resistance movement in Gaza and the West Bank, although these areas had once appeared most promising. Increasingly, the center of fedayeen military activity was pulled back, first to the Jordan valley, and, after Karameh, still even further away from the Israeli frontier. The fedayeen came to depend on hit-and-run commando raids with brutally high casualty rates. Yet the fedayeen continued announcing one triumph after another. While

---

[15] *Free Palestine*, vol. 2, no. 1 (June 1969).
[16] Y. Harkabi, "Fedayeen Action and Arab Strategy," *Adelphi Papers* (London), no. 53 (December 1968), pp. 14-15.

these "triumphs" were invisible to neutral observers, in an Arab world starved for victories, fedayeen stature and influence soared. In January 1969, even Nasser lavished praise on the new heroes, at whose disposal he unconditionally placed all the resources of the UAR.

For the next twenty months, the fedayeen often seemed the dominant factor in any Middle East equation. Winning the hearts of the Arab masses, they had gained a virtual veto power over the policies of the Arab regimes and even threatened the existence of the Lebanese and Jordanian governments. They received the adulation of the international radicals, and the world's press and television riveted their attention on fedayeen activities. Undeniably the fedayeen had revitalized the Palestine issue. Yet their strategy of guerrilla revolution as a means to power had been a military disaster, so much so that by the summer of 1970 the fedayeen were no longer even a marginal military threat to Israeli security. A few fedayeen leaders recognized this military failure, but many continued to live in an atmosphere of euphoria in which a dramatic communiqué or a television interview hid military disasters.

The PFLP. Of all the various competing fedayeen subgroups, the most militantly revolutionary from the first were the descendents of the Arab National Movement founded by George Habash. Before 1967 Habash had regarded al Fatah as a parochial, Palestinian, middle-class effort. By the end of 1967, however, Habash had been converted to the al Fatah guerrilla strategy and had organized the Popular Front for the Liberation of Palestine (PFLP)—a group that in turn would splinter off into other new fronts. Habash, unlike the other fedayeen leaders, insisted not only on the ultimate necessity of general revolution, at least throughout the Arab world, but also on the need to adopt other tactics than the popular guerrilla techniques. He argued that Zionism should be attacked everywhere and with any effective means. Consequently, PFLP agents within Israel organized bomb attacks on targets chosen not for their military value but for maximum terrorist impact—bus stations, the Hebrew University, a supermarket, and a cafe.

However, like the other fedayeen groups, the PFLP soon found that it was nearly impossible to maintain its cells for very long or to replace lost members. An alternative tactic was devised. On 23 July 1968, a three-man PFLP team took over an El Al Boeing 707 soon after takeoff from Rome. Instead of landing at Tel Aviv, the plane arrived in Algeria, to the delight of much of the Arab world and the dismay of the Israelis. This was the first example of the PFLP's new direction. On 26 December 1968, two fedayeen attacked an El Al plane on the ground at Athens, killing one Israeli.

While the international community seemed content with polite protest—even though Arab governments appeared guilty of collusion—the Israelis were outraged. Because Lebanon had been the point of origin for both PFLP operations, Israel struck back at the Beirut airport on 28 December. A helicopter-borne commando group blew up fourteen planes belonging to Arab airlines and retired untouched to Israel. The cycle of terror, provocation, and retaliation had begun—a cycle that would lead to assassinations, bombings, and other spectacular and appalling incidents. El Al offices were attacked throughout Europe and El Al planes became prime targets. Because the United States was a supporter of Israel, in August 1969 a TWA aircraft was hijacked to Damascus and blown up on the ground. Soon after this incident, a PFLP splinter group, the PFLP General Command, planted a bomb on a Swissair jet bound for Israel. The plane exploded over Switzerland, killing forty-seven people, sixteen of them Israelis.

Black September. The PFLP's most spectacular operation was carried out in September 1970. It transformed the Middle East balance and provoked a civil war in Jordan that nearly eviscerated all the fedayeen movements. On 6 September PFLP attack teams in Europe took command of four New York-bound jets soon after takeoff. One plane was directed to Beirut, where nine fedayeen came aboard and wired the first-class cabin with explosives. This plane was then flown to Cairo, where, in protest against Egyptian acceptance of the American secretary of state's proposal for a peace initiative, it was blown up.

The PFLP had different plans for the other jets. These would provide hostages for an unprecedented exercise in international bargaining. The Swissair and TWA jets were directed to Dawson Field, an old British airstrip north of Amman in Jordan. The El Al plane did not join them because the takeover attempt had collapsed, with one fedayeen killed and the other, Leila Khaled (who had already succeeded in hijacking a TWA plane to Damascus the previous year), captured. Despite this setback, the PFLP had two jets and 310 hostages securely on the ground. When the PFLP discovered that against all odds there were no British nationals aboard the two planes, they simply hijacked a BOAC VC-10 on its way to Beirut and added it to the array at Dawson Field.

The PFLP communiqué called for the release of Leila Khaled, three guerrillas held by West Germany, three held in Switzerland, and an unspecified number held by Israel. On the following morning, with the field ringed by units of the Jordanian army, the long drama began, as the various governments concerned sought to make the best of a bad bargain. By the time the BOAC aircraft arrived on 9 September, sporadic firing had begun between the fedayeen and the Jordanian army. As the days passed and hectic negotiations continued, these incidents grew more frequent and Jordanian patience evaporated. On 12 September, the jets were blown up by the PFLP. Shooting between the Jordanian army and the fedayeen in Amman grew more general in the days after the three planes were destroyed. Then a new and largely military Jordanian cabinet took over, determined to crush the fedayeen.

In the midst of the chaos, with some hostages released and some not, the frantic bargaining continued. The violent repression by the Jordanian army rapidly produced an intense crisis, with the brief intervention of the Syrian army and the prospect of great-power involvement. On 27 September, President Nasser managed to negotiate a truce between the shattered fedayeen forces and King Hussein. (It was the Egyptian president's last political act, for he collapsed and died the following day.) The remaining hostages were released, and true to the promises made during the negotiations, the various governments freed the fedayeen prisoners, including Leila Khaled.

This incident fundamentally altered worldwide perception of the Palestine Liberation Movement. Millions of people, who had watched the destruction of the three huge planes on television, now knew not only of the Palestinian issue but also of the vulnerability of the international community to the tactics of terror. The Dawson Field spectacular had profoundly reduced fedayeen potential and stature. During the month of fighting—Black September—King Hussein's army had largely wiped out any Jordanian fedayeen sanctuary, so that even the most sanguine in al Fatah recognized that guerrilla operations could no longer originate in Jordan. The experience of the next few months proved that this was largely true in Lebanon as well.

The fedayeen strategy of revolutionary guerrilla war lay in a shambles. The PFLP insisted that the guerrilla campaign had never been the best strategy and that only continued attacks on targets outside Israel would destroy Zionism and imperialism. In fact, an increasing number of fedayeen accepted that the *only* effective means to act on events would be by recourse to such operations. Harried out of their sanctuaries and restricted to the camps, the Palestinians felt that the only alternative to resignation and despair was to continue the "armed struggle" through terror. Israel and the Zionists might prove invulnerable for the time being, but at least the anguish of Palestine would not be ignored. A shadowy umbrella organization known as Black September evolved out of this fedayeen anguish and joined the PFLP in pursuing the new strategy.[17] On 29 November, Jordanian Prime Minister Wasfi Tal was assassinated as he left the lobby of the Cairo Sheraton. The next month an attempt on the life of the Jordanian ambassador to Britain barely failed. Vengeance at least was possible, and many Palestinians continued to feel that Jordan under Hussein was as great an enemy as Israel. As Israel appeared increasingly out of reach, the fedayeen had to seek elsewhere for targets. A Lufthansa jet was hijacked to Aden and released for a $5 million ransom in February 1972. Next a Sabena jet was seized by four terrorists and flown into Israel's Lod Airport, where Israeli security agents killed two of the fedayeen and captured the other two. Several bombing attempts on El Al planes were unsuccessful, and Israeli agents were taking a quiet toll of fedayeen operatives throughout Europe in what was known as the "spooks' war."

On 30 May 1972, at Lod Airport three Japanese passengers suddenly pulled automatic weapons and grenades from their luggage and opened fire into a crowded waiting room. Within minutes the gunfire and grenades left twenty-five persons dead—including eleven Puerto Rican Christians on a religious pilgrimage to the Holy Land—and fifty-nine wounded. Before they could be captured, one of the Japanese committed suicide with a grenade, while in the confusion another was shot down by one of his colleagues. The remaining Japanese, Kozo Okamoto, had been captured. All three had been trained and armed by the PFLP and sent into Lod as living tools of destruction. The three were members of *Rengo Sekigum* (the Red Army), a tiny Japanese movement possessed of a poetic vision and dedicated to world revolution.[18] At his trial, Kozo Okamoto explained that both executioners and victims,

---

[17] The Israelis contend that Black September is simply a branch of al Fatah that has from time to time recruited from other groups for specific operations. Reputedly the key figure is Abu Ayad, but published details have remained vague.
[18] The Red Army's most unsavory operation was the murder of fourteen of their own militants during a purge in 1972.

united in death, would be reincarnated as stars whose light would shed eternal peace on earth. Such an explanation made the attack seem more like a natural catastrophe than a rational act of man.[19]

In many ways the Lod massacre was the most frightening and ominous of the long series of fedayeen terror operations, particularly because of the use of surrogate operatives—Japanese who seemed almost eager to sacrifice their lives in what should have been an alien cause. The horror of this bizarre incident sent waves of concern and discontent rippling through an international community increasingly feeling the fedayeen threat. As had long been suspected, the Arabs obviously had contacts with other militants throughout the world. As had also been suspected, there appeared to be little limit to the ruthlessness of their operations. Even more important, the targets of the fedayeen had now become so random and imprecisely defined that anyone might be endangered. Standing in the wrong queue or before the wrong ticket booth was enough to qualify one as an ally of Zionism. The Lod massacre implied that to fedayeen eyes the web of international order contained so many potentially "Zionist" strands that conventional security could no longer be guaranteed to travelers or, perhaps, to anyone else.

On 5 September 1972, eight Black September fedayeen rushed the headquarters of the Israeli Olympic team in Munich, seized the athletes as hostages, and opened another round of bargaining. This time the hostages were not as fortunate as those at Dawson Field. When German security forces attempted to free them before they were to board the escape plane provided by the Bonn government, the operation collapsed into a chaos of gunfire and grenade explosions. Eleven Israelis and five Black September fedayeen were killed. Three fedayeen were captured. The following month, Black September seized a Lufthansa plane en route between Beirut and Ankara, flew it into Zagreb, and demanded the release of the three. The Germans quickly complied. For Black September, Munich had been a remarkable success, forcing renewed world attention to the Palestine issue. The point had been made: There can be no peace, not even at the Olympics,

---

[19] In Beirut, the spokesman for the PFLP, Ghassan Kanafani, defended the operation (*Washington Post*, 9 July 1972): "Our style of operation is not an invention of one person but a result of our situation. If we could liberate Palestine by standing on the borders of South Lebanon and throwing roses on the Israelis we would do it. It is nicer. But I don't think it will work." A little over a month later Kanafani was killed when his sports car exploded on a Beirut street. The Israelis had no comment.

while justice is denied the Palestinians. If the world was disgusted, this was so much the better—everyone now knew how to eliminate the need for such operations in the future.[20]

In December 1972, the fedayeen took over the Israeli embassy in Bangkok, seizing six hostages. This time, after intricate negotiations, the fedayeen were allowed to fly out of the country after having released the hostages without gain. In order to regain credibility after this fiasco, Black September choreographed still another spectacular. They planned an operation in Khartoum which would challenge Sudanese President Ja'far al-Numairi. Numairi had pursued several policies distasteful to the fedayeen. He had come to an agreement with the southern Sudanese rebels, who had been aided by Israel, and had alienated Colonel Muammar Qaddafi of Libya, the fedayeen's most loyal supporter. The fedayeen hoped to present Numairi with a series of unpleasant options, realizing that under any circumstances, much of Sudanese opinion would be on their side. The specific setting of this mission would be the Saudi Arabian embassy, so as to punish, or at least embarrass, the fedayeen's Arab opponents. The target would be Western diplomats, the active agents of "Western-Zionist imperialism." Finally, once bargaining began, there would be no such easy deals as had spoiled the effort in Bangkok. Unless every demand was met almost at once, the hostages would be killed. And the fedayeen knew that such total and immediate concessions would be unlikely. This was to be a killing mission, after which Black September would once again be taken seriously.

On 1 March 1973, they carried out their occupation of the Saudi embassy and seized the new American ambassador, Cleo Noel, the former American chargé, Curt Moore, and the Belgian chargé, Guy Eid, at a farewell reception for Moore. The guests, servants, and most of the diplomats were released, but the "enemies" were kept—along with the Saudi ambassador and the Jordanian chargé. The fedayeen presented a shopping list of demands, to which President Nixon responded: "We will do everything we can to get them released but we will not pay blackmail." [21] Sudanese intermediaries attempted unsuccessfully to find

---

[20] After the Munich incident in September 1972, a Palestinian spokesman (Abu Ahmed) noted that "they never cared about us. Why should we care about them?"—"them" being the outraged West (*New York Times*, 20 September 1972): "Call us what you may but it's good for our morale, and it may help the moderate elements in the movement to take a more militant position. After all our defeats, this comes as an uplift. We feel we have to do something. What does the world expect of young Arabs these days? We have seen too many defeats."

[21] *New York Times*, 3 March 1972.

a solution satisfactory to the fedayeen. On 3 March, negotiations collapsed and the fedayeen shot and killed the three Western diplomats—Noel, Moore, and Eid—and then surrendered to Sudanese authorities. There were few after that who did not take Black September very seriously indeed.

The Splinter Groups. The terror strategy of Black September/PFLP increasingly appealed to other less organized fedayeen, who now saw the vulnerability of an airport waiting room or an embassy. Here and there ad hoc groups with romantic names coalesced and dissolved around the prospect of action. Arms, funds, and sanctuary were available despite repeated disclaimers from most Arab regimes and nearly all reputable Arab spokesmen. And so the cycle of terror and response continued; there were attacks on El Al planes on the ground, a machine-gun attack on a crowded airport waiting room in Athens,[22] and a plot to shoot down an El Al jet with a SAM-7 missile was reported in Rome.

One of the most effective efforts came at the end of September 1973, when two fedayeen from the previously unknown Eagles of the Palestine Revolution raided a Moscow-to-Vienna train and took three Soviet Jews and an Austrian customs official as hostages. The fedayeen said they would release the Austrian if they were permitted to fly out of the Vienna airport with their three Jewish hostages. Austrian Chancellor Bruno Kreisky turned down that demand, but offered as an alternative a promise to close down Schonau Castle, the Jewish transit facility, and allow the fedayeen to leave the country in return for all four hostages. To this the delighted fedayeen agreed. They flew off to ovations from nearly every Arab source,[23] as President Anwar Sadat of Egypt immediately sent a special representative, Ismail Fahmy, to Vienna to thank Kreisky for closing the transit camp. In response, Golda Meir personally traveled to Vienna to urge Kreisky to reconsider, but without

---

[22] On 24 January 1974, the two fedayeen were sentenced to death, a sentence few thought would be carried out given the Greek government's willingness to release them in December at the request of the Rome hijackers. Either the Greeks hoped to make a deal with the fedayeen to respect Greek neutrality or anticipated an almost certain hostage-seizing operation that would rid them of the two, similar to the pro forma exercise that freed the Munich fedayeen. And this proved to be the case; the fedayeen seized a Greek ship and Athens released the Arabs. By one means or another most captured fedayeen are released.

[23] There had been a series of blunders and aborted attempts before the successful one—a success that the fedayeen had not foreseen, although subsequently spokesmen contended even a computer had been used in planning the operation to ensure its success.

success. Her complaints gave the Arabs even more satisfaction. She argued that:

> There must be no relenting on the demand placed on the Government of Austria that it rescind the promise made to terrorists under pressure of threats and violence.
>
> This promise constitutes a serious infringement of the foundations of morality and international law and is liable to encourage additional acts of violence.[24]

During the October War, which began only a few days later, attention shifted to the conventional violence that overshadowed the fedayeen. But in November, as soon as the fighting had ended, an unknown band of fedayeen, the Arab National Youth Organization, seized a KLM jet, chosen because the Dutch had supposedly sided with Israel during the October War. These fedayeen wandered through five different airports while carrying on confused and uncertain bargaining with the Dutch government. Ultimately, the Dutch agreed to ban transporting weapons or volunteers to Israel and noted that Holland was not involved in the transporting of Soviet Jews to Israel or in giving aid to Israel. Some Arab observers saw this as another victory—concessions wrung from the pro-Zionist Dutch. For nearly everyone else the exercise had been a futile sideshow. The major thrust of Middle Eastern events could be found elsewhere.

Desperation. By November it was clear that a serious American effort, apparently with Russian acquiescence, was going to be made to find a solution that would prevent further rounds of violence in the Middle East. The Palestinian fedayeen suspected, not without reason, that any or all of the Arab regimes might well sell them out. Except for Qadaffi, who hated the idea of negotiations, most Arab regimes felt bolstered by the strong military showing during the war and the impact of the oil embargo, believing they could negotiate from a position of strength. Fear of betrayal, however, led some of the more desperate fedayeen to prepare a new operation. Rumors circulated of a plot with Libyan support to assassinate Henry Kissinger when he arrived in Beirut on 16 December. No attempt took place; and on 16 January 1974 Libya issued a statement denying the allegation:

> The Libyan Arab Republic is a state with a moral obligation, where a popular revolution took place, embodying the

---

[24] *New York Times*, 4 October 1973.

highest cherished human principles, value and ideals, advocating the theory of universal rights and justice for all mankind.

Therefore, it is ridiculous to accuse the Libyan Arab Republic of being behind an assassination plan against anybody. Such accusations are naked heresays, motivated by ignorance, hatred, grudge and racial and religious bigotry.[25]

No matter what Libya's position, observers believed that if the diplomatic negotiations began to bear fruit the militant fedayeen would have no option but to protest through a new spectacular deed. In January 1974 Europe was alive with rumors of an impending terrorist offensive. These were apparently of sufficient substance to persuade many governments to tighten up airport security. The British even sent troops and armor to Heathrow Airport on full-scale alert. Although 1974 saw a decline in the number of fedayeen operations, suicide raids on Israeli settlements caused grave concern. No one was ready to conclude that the militant fedayeen intended to discard their strategy of terror.[26] When Yassir Arafat, al Fatah's leader, addressed the United Nations, he gave no indication that the Palestinians had changed their goals. For the unrepentant and dedicated fedayeen, any mini–West Bank Palestine established by diplomatic agreement with the forces of Zionism is anathema: "When prophecy fails there are two possibilities, you resign yourself to reality—or you become more fanatical." [27] Many frustrated and desperate Palestinians are committed to the latter course.

Summary. The Palestinian fedayeen have produced the most spectacular modern deeds of terrorist violence. Of all rebels, they have become, perhaps, the most desperate. In early 1970, despite the dismal returns from the battlefield, the fedayeen continued to assume that at last they would punish the arrogance of Zionism and that their victory was certain. By the end of the year, decimated by Hussein's repression, all revolutionary euphoria had vanished and the guerrilla campaign was over. The only option available was a strategy of terror. Thus, although the conventional elements of the Arab world expressed horror, most

---

25 *New York Times,* 18 January 1974.

26 At the end of the month the Red Army/PFLP struck again, this time in Singapore, where an attempt to sabotage Shell Oil installations failed. The four terrorists involved then seized a ferryboat and hostages and began negotiations to trade for Japanese diplomats and free passage to an unnamed Arab country. Ultimately the Japanese embassy in Kuwait was seized, the fedayeen brought from Singapore, exchanged for the diplomatic hostages, and flown on to Aden.

27 *New York Times,* 20 September 1972.

Palestinians recognized the meaning of the massacres. Terror was the only means of action available, the only escape from utter impotence. In this, Black September's experience paralleled that of Lehi when it had faced dissolution. Black September, however, had not initiated the strategy of terror, but had copied Habash and the PFLP.

Habash had initiated terror tactics in the avowed pursuit of a multi-faceted attack on Israel. The PFLP was too weak to organize a major guerrilla offensive inside the occupied zone and thus took recourse to spectacular terrorist operations in order to increase the organization's visibility. To succeed in gaining such visibility, Habash had to find an ideological strategy more radical than that of al Fatah. This explains the elaborate ideological justifications it issued in explanation of its strategy of skyjacking. In a sense, the PFLP, more than the other fedayeen group, recognized the basic military weakness of the Palestinians vis-à-vis Israel. By 1969 it had become almost impossible for the leadership of the PFLP to continue to pretend that the Arabs were winning. In the case of the PFLP, and later Black September, a strategy of terror was chosen only when the vision of revolutionary victory collapsed. As long as there was no hope of "conventional" victory, that is, before October 1973, nearly all the fedayeen privately accepted the need to continue such objectionable means, even if Arab opinion would be alienated. After the October War an increasing number of Palestinians hoped that at least they might gain half a loaf—a small state on the West Bank of the Jordan. As always, the ultra-militants wanted complete success.

Despite a common revolutionary vocation, the Irish volunteer, the African nationalist, the Argentine Trotskyite, and the Arab fedayeen act within very different traditions and pursue aspirations similar only in their opposition to existing order. They select their tactics and strategy for special and often personal reasons. Such men, often dedicated to a transcendental vision and impelled by past failure or present impotence, resort to terror not as an isolated tactic, but as a comprehensive strategy.

3

Transnational Terror

Revolutionary Terror: Prospects

Barring some unique transformation in the nature of man or his institutions, transnational terror and revolutionary violence will be with us in the future, just as they have been with us for centuries past. Even in relatively stable, democratic, developed societies, events of the last decade revealed schisms that have produced mobs, bombings, and even gunfire in the streets. Even advanced authoritarian regimes with the resources and will to repress ruthlessly any open dissent have not always been able to impose order. In some cases, political frustration can be accommodated. This has been done in democratic societies by peaceful political means and in authoritarian societies by other, repressive means. Generally, in industrialized countries, conventional accommodation permits either concessions or the surety of repression, and, of course, failure deters even the most militant. But frustration may be so galling that a few will stand violent witness, for no one can ever be *sure* a cause is hopeless.

The most significant exception to the general revolutionary reticence under such circumstances has been the violence generated by separatist rebels in the name of a submerged or incomplete nation; the Basques, Kurds, Bretons, Irish, Tyrol, Germans, Jurassiens, Croatians, and even the Ukrainians have not given up hope. Generally, even in these cases, an armed struggle can be maintained only where accommodation is beyond the capacity or desire of the established system, where a revolutionary victory, if not certain, at least seems possible, and where rationally deployed violence can be seen to have an effect.

69

Beyond the bounds of postindustrial society and in certain tension spots within it lies a vast other world, where more often than not small groups of elites struggle with competing and urgent priorities. They must rely on fragile central institutions to effect a modernization that regularly eludes them. Such regimes appear to many not only unjust but vulnerable. Even the most stable third world societies making demonstrable progress towards modernization and with secure central power have not been beyond the ambitions of rebels: Naxalites in India, Marighella's urban guerrillas in Brazil, and the Dev-Genc in Turkey. Thus, in recent years in scores of nations, a rebel band has been able to maintain armed defiance. Never attaining the hoped-for victory, but never submitting to complete defeat, in nearly every country where such groups have appeared they have survived. But only in Cuba have the rebels come down out of the hills and into a deserted presidential palace. The enthusiasm of most revolutionaries can not overcome their impotence. The desire to be a guerrilla has at times divorced the rebel from reality and led him to pursue his dream into a world of fantasy. The advocates of Guevara's *foco* theory often found themselves isolated from the local peasants, who proved not only hostile but often spoke Indian languages unknown to the rebels. Such *focoistas* provided the loyal military forces with live targets, but not with a viable revolutionary challenge. There have, however, been sufficient successes—such as the Portuguese collapse—to encourage other rebels. The failure of guerrilla revolution, even when employed against fragile or odious regimes, has not deterred the many rebels who contend that the struggle can build a new nation, that new men, purged by violence of servility *à la* Fanon, will emerge from the guerrilla cauldron. The result has been that the new guerrilla revolutionaries place great emphasis on mass mobilization and the pursuit of an armed struggle that, if irregular, is recognizably "military." Thus, these leaders have not emphasized terror tactics. Even those who *do* employ the techniques of terror in the course of their armed struggle often choose local targets. The major thrust of contemporary revolutionary activity has been towards guerrilla strategy, urban or rural, focused narrowly on the target regime, rather than on the international system or distant secondary opponents. Those who rely largely on the tactics of terror, and who export their operations, have in the last generation been an exception—but a most spectacular exception. What is disturbing for the threatened is that the techniques of terror produce sensational impact and have thereby attracted not only the criminal and the demented, but even rebels who, without the media exposure always given to terrorist activity, might have remained ignorant of the potential for such operations. Instead of tending their own barren revolutionary gardens, some have broadened their tactical arsenal, adopting some of the least unsavory techniques.

Still, even with the spread of terrorist techniques and tactics, there has not yet been a rush to challenge the entire transnational system. Even though the United States and other Western nations are often identified by contemporary revolutionaries as the directors of an exploitive system, the activists, with a few notable exceptions, have stayed within national bounds. This reticence to venture abroad may be only a passing phase. The Latin American rebels who have been repeatedly frustrated by their failure to emulate Castro—or even to maintain their resistance—may seek out other targets.

It must be remembered that—again, with a few notable exceptions—revolutionaries are driven, desperate men. They are pursued and harassed, and seldom have time for reflection or planning. The result has been what might be called institutionalized revolutionary incompetence.[1] The number of fedayeen operations bungled are legion, and the incapacities of the IRA are legendary. Thus what makes transnational order so vulnerable is not the capability of the terrorist, but the complexity of the system. Even if it is clumsily tossed, a wrench in the wrong place can seriously damage the transnational machine. To prevent the murder of diplomats or the hijacking of airplanes—operations clearly within the grasp of even the most incompetent—requires a vast allocation of resources. It is thus fortunate that most potential terrorists do not have the capability to devise more sophisticated threats. In November 1973, for example, an attempt was made to extort 21 million marks from the West German government by threatening to spread anthrax and botulism through the mail or public water supplies. Though there appear to be but a limited number of trained scientists among

---

[1] The major factors that result in revolutionary incompetence may be (1) the increasing assumption of responsibility by the talented to the point of overload and (2) the inherent nature of all conspiracy that hinders internal communication, often thereby guaranteeing rising incomprehension within the organization, hardening disagreement, and ultimately schism. Then, too, revolutionaries are pressed for time and thus opt for the possible and familiar—one car bomb leads to another. Even shifting tactical directions is often very difficult, and big decisions and actions are quite rare. Finally many revolutionaries are hampered by an unwillingness to act opportunistically, preferring not simply the familiar but also what in theory is appropriate. A good many rebels have had a bad fate because the book they read proved to be the wrong one.

71

terrorist organizations, it would take only one such incident to produce a calamity. Naturally, no one wants to depend for protection on revolutionary incompetence or the whims of fate, particularly in an era in which there are growing indications of worldwide cooperation among revolutionary groups.

Transnational Revolution:
Conspiracy, Collusion, and Cooperation

There has been several incidents of either proven or suspected cooperation between revolutionary groups in different countries. For example, on 20 December 1973, thirteen suspected revolutionaries—ten Turks, two Palestinians, and one Algerian—were arrested in Villiers-Sur-Marne, forty-eight miles east of Paris. The French police announced that the Turks, members of the Popular Liberation Front of Turkey, had been trained by the Arabs in revolutionary warfare. On 29 December of the same year, at Heathrow Airport in Britain, an American woman allegedly possessing arms and ammunition was arrested along with a Moroccan who met her. Two days later a Pakistani associate was also arrested upon his arrival at Heathrow. British police indicated that the Moroccan belonged to a group seeking to overthrow King Hassan II. On 3 January 1974, an unnamed British intelligence official indicated that the IRA and the Arabs had agreed to cooperate in launching terror operations in Britain. In France, the Breton Liberation Front has cooperated with the IRA and the Basque ETA separatist movement. The mix of Turks, Arabs, Moroccans, and Americans in these incidents underscored fears in various official quarters that a real if not fully formed transnational revolutionary conspiracy existed.

The most dramatic evidence of this trend was the 1972 Lod Airport massacre in Israel. Members of the Japanese *Renyo Sikigum* performed the deed in behalf of the PFLP. When Arab fedayeen were apprehended and condemned to death after an operation in Athens, their release was sought by three Philippine members of the Moslem International Guerrillas (a group previously active in the Philippines and Indonesia). They seized the Greek freighter *Voei* in Karachi and held two hostages until the Greek government agreed to commute the death sentences. Athens soon thereafter released the two Black September fedayeen, although the government insisted that this release had been planned all along and had not been related to the seizure of the freighter. Both fedayeen operations revealed extensive transnational cooperation against what was apparently seen as a common opponent.

Elsewhere there was evidence that Palestinian guerrillas had received aid and comfort, from local revolutionaries during or before operations in Trieste and Germany. In fact, for many years the activities of the several Palestinian fedayeen groups had attracted volunteers with varying Arab backgrounds and even a few non-Arabs, but operational cooperation with revolutionary organizations elsewhere has been rare. Such alliances have occurred between like-minded revolutionaries in the past. They were used primarily for propaganda purposes and took the form of liberation committees, guerrilla summits, and regional alignments. Several of the Latin American revolutionary *foco,* most notably Che Guevara's in Bolivia, had foreign volunteers. At various times Cubans were involved in the Congo, and Eritreans have trained in Syria. Still, for a generation most contemporary revolutionary organizations have been bounded by national borders, even while sharing to varying degrees an international ideology.

There have always existed centers of world revolution offering a special ideological strategy and granting seals of approval to distant advocates of the "true way." In the last decade, the three prime advocates of revolution have been Cuba, Communist China, and Russia. Though each is a center of a net of rebels, the efforts of the sponsored groups are usually directed at a specific nation. All efforts to construct a single international revolutionary umbrella organization have broken on various ideological rocks and the self-interest of the competing centers. The only durable alliance has been the Organization of the Solidarity of the Peoples of Africa, Asia, and Latin America. Founded in Havana in January 1966, this body has evolved into little more than an anti-Chinese Marxist-Leninist publicity bureau and convention center.

Far more important than the various world or regional fronts have been the advocacy and encouragement of revolution by established governments on both ideological and pragmatic grounds. In the years immediately after Castro's success in Cuba, his new regime supported and often sponsored revolutionary expeditions throughout Latin America, hoping to spread the new gospel and reduce Cuba's isolation. In recent years, however, the old revolutionary centers have increasingly abandoned overt subversion, preferring to deal directly with existing governments, except where liberation struggles oppose generally unpopular opponents—as in the recent case of Portugal. In an era of détente, even the Chinese appear less enthusiastic about sponsoring revolution. Some of the slack has been taken up by militant Arab regimes, with often curious results. At one point Libya was making use of the South Yemeni island of Kamaran to trans-ship arms to the Eritrean Liberation Front in Ethiopia, while simultaneously supplying equipment to groups dedicated to the overthrow of the South Yemeni "Communist" regime. In any case, such webs of subversion do not quite add up to a transnational structure of revolution.

If there is not a single world revolutionary organization, but rather a collection of competing groups, fronts, and alliances, many active revolutionaries are convinced that a world revolutionary comradeship exists. It may be a band of quarreling brothers, but it is a band nevertheless. Besides the widespread alliance to the lineage of revolutionary ideologists and strategists, rebels everywhere feel a solidarity with others waging armed struggle against colonialism or neo-imperialism. Even the most parochial of rebels, such as the Kurds or the Basques, soon develop an international posture and feel akin to distant rebels who employ similar strategies and share the same heroes. Distance may strengthen bonds that intimacy might have frayed; but while such connections may improve morale, they cannot effect military efficiency.

On a regional rather than a worldwide level, considerable effort towards cooperation has been made by revolutionaries who share the same or similar opponents. In Africa some of those opposed to the Portuguese came together in the Conference of National Organizations in the Portuguese Colonies, but to no great effect. Among several other alliances, perhaps most viable has been an alignment of African liberation movements sharing similar ideological postures and sponsors. Cooperating groups have included the African National Congress (ANC) (South Africa), the Zimbabwe African People's Union (ZAPU) (Rhodesia), the *Movimento Popular de Libertacão Angola,* the *Frente de Libertacao de Mocambique,* the *Partido Africano da Independência da Guine e Cabo Verde*, and the South-West Africa People's Organization. The most intimate cooperation in the field was a joint ANC-ZAPU guerrilla incursion in August 1967 across the Zambezi River near Victoria Falls, which aborted when it was discovered by Rhodesian security forces.

In the Middle East, the Palestinian fedayeen have found cooperation even more elusive than have the Africans. The recognized Palestinian umbrella organization, the PLO, seldom covers all the divided and wrangling groups that represent nearly every ideological current in the Arab Middle East and advocate varying and often contradictory revolutionary strategies. At least the various trans-Arab movements like the Baathist or the Arab National Movement provide a unifying revolutionary influence in the Middle East. But, for the most part, regional cooperation for revolution has been hindered by the clash of ideology which creates competing subversive webs pursuing alternative strategies.

The rifts and schisms within the revolutionary world do not prevent ad hoc cooperation in certain areas, as, for example, the PFLP–*Rengo Sekigum* alliance, which clearly went beyond simple regional arrangements. There are, however, severe obstacles to the widespread duplication of this example. To adjust Arab tactical needs to those of the revolutionaries of other countries is a more complex problem than agreeing on a common imperialist foe and a similar revolutionary strategy.

In sum, there is not a single transnational conspiracy against order; there are not even several regional conspiracies. Rather there is a revolutionary medium or milieu that permits and encourages the exchange of aid and comfort between parties as diverse as Basques and Turks, Irish and Arabs. The prospect is that there will continue to be contacts and cooperation between groups, but there is little likelihood that a viable world conspiracy will coalesce.

Sponsored Terror. A more serious challenge to order may come from rebels sponsored by ruling regimes with denied ambitions. Assured of sanctuary and support, a rebel can be less cautious and more daring and can draw upon broader resources. Such support, particularly the prospect of sanctuary, makes the revolutionary far more effective and dangerous. In the past, concerted international action to prevent sponsorship has always been difficult, and such favored options as a pilots' boycott to end skyjacking or embargoes on necessities have seldom proved effective. Open battle against the sponsoring states carries grave risks and, as the Israelis discovered, is not the final solution. Alien funds and foreign agitators have, of course, been used to stir up previously peaceful inhabitants for centuries, but in trying to draw conclusions about such actions, one finds that each case is different. Fortunately, times change and enthusiasms ebb. Other national priorities may arise or discreet pressures may finally persuade a sponsor to withhold support. For now, the growing reluctance of prospective host regimes to accept the poisoned parcel of a hijacked airliner is encouraging, but the lack of regular extradition of hijackers remains most disheartening.

The Transnational Medium. With or without the sponsorship or acquiescence of ruling regimes, transnational terror appears to be a growth field. It sometimes seems as if each operation encourages the next, and many rebels are increasingly reluctant to deny themselves the terror option. There is evidence that the entire transnational system may have become a new violence zone, a legitimate target for revolutionary operations.

In each local violence zone, differing tactics might well become sanctioned by usage as recognized means of political action. In Ireland, the shooting of policemen has become recognized as a political act, even though in another country the same action would be seen as criminal, no matter what political explanation was proffered. Most Americans regard Black Liberation Army rationalizations for the vicious and almost mindless murder of innocent policemen as feeble excuses. There may also be certain conventions in given violence zones, such as limitation on targets, giving of fair warning, or the prescription of killing. In 1947, for example, it was always possible to recognize from the description of resistance operations in Palestine the hand of the Haganah, Irgun, or Lehi by the degree of restraint. Obviously, these revolutionary restraints tend not to be stable over time.

The shift to transnational terror and away from guerrilla revolution is as yet a slight one, and remains a maneuver of the truly desperate. The turn to terror is the result of a complex confluence of forces including: (1) the regular failure of revolutionary campaigns in the third world which have produced only escalated repression, (2) the repeated collapse of other new strategies, (3) the recognition of the potential for exploitation of the mass media, and (4) political trends within the third world. With the end of overt colonial rule, third world nationalists may begin to look towards the ultimate sources of imperialism. They see the world as controlled by an imperialist-capitalist-racist conspiracy of vast power, immune to conventional revolutionary strategies. Because of the new complexities of the powerful postindustrial world, the rebel can strike and strike hard at what he sees as an evil system, even if he cannot change it. Thus some revolutionaries have moved into transnational terror. There is no reason to suppose that present revolutionaries will in the immediate future shift their assumptions or lose their aspirations.

It must also be remembered that the system under terrorist attack is remarkably stable, while the revolutionaries remain remarkably feeble. Terrorist incidents may produce horror and indignation, but actual systemic disruption is minimal. Airlines still fly, passengers still wait in transit lounges, and the cargo gets through. Major cities withstood much more devastating assaults in World War II than could ever be managed by terrorists. London was bombed every day for months, and Germany, with vast areas reduced to rubble, managed to increase aircraft production almost until the end of the war. The real effect of terrorist action on the transnational system will always be more a matter of appearance than of reality. The toll of the terrorist is more comparable to the rate of auto fatalities than to the slaughter of conventional war. Even in Northern Ireland, more people die on the highways than by terror.

The system, far from being rigid, is in truth amply pliable and can absorb the various terrorist threats. There is a variety of defenses as well as a mix of responses possible, but because of the dread nature of these new revolutionary acts, the general reaction has been deeply emotional rather than practical. This vast indignation provides a poor foundation for what is clearly going to be a continuing and perhaps escalating assault on world order.

4

The American Response

The almost universal reaction to most terrorist spectaculars has been horror, incomprehension, and indignation:

> The feral Arab guerrillas who were responsible for yesterday's carnage have not been identified at the time of writing. Even in an age which has supped more than its fill of blood and violence, this mass-killing by flame and bullet can have no half-way sane defenders. It is impossible, at first shock, to understand what these murderers thought they were achieving. . . . Condemnation of the murderers is worldwide, and they have no claim on sanctuary: any Government which tried to shelter such rabid creatures would surely find itself internationally ostracised.

This immediate editorial response of the *Irish Times* to the 17 December 1973 Rome massacre was part of the worldwide horror and repulsion at the "mindless" murder of the innocent by hysterical and "irrational criminals." The horror was not quite universal, however, for despite the official Arab disclaimers, legitimate regimes, unlike terrorists, do have to consider at times their image and the prospect of retaliation by the injured. Many in the Middle East understood and approved of the fedayeen's motives. After all, during October thousands of Arabs had been killed by weapons made in America, and hence to some degree all American individuals and institutions were thought to bear some guilt. And Kuwait did *not* rush to extradite the fedayeen to Rome or to try them. The massacre may have been barbarous, but so had been the treatment dealt out to the Palestinians for a generation. So the Kuwaitis waited. Security for the diplomats engaged in the Middle East peace negotiations was tightened. International attention ebbed. And little changed. Procedures at Rome airport—and at London's Heathrow and Paris's Orly—were adjusted to prevent a recurrence of the incident. The demands for an end to sanctuary may here or there have impressed some governments. Mainly, however, the world went on its way, vulnerable to the next spectacular that, too, would generate horror and disgust and, if the past were prologue, little else.

In formulating a strategy of response, American policy makers must begin by examining the record of the many anti-terrorist efforts that have been waged by other governments. Among the target regimes most severely threatened, there has over the previous decade been a variety of responses to provocation, ranging from authorized counter-terror through vigilantism, in addition to full reliance on existing procedures and traditional legal responses. The Ethiopian government, for example, took an exceedingly dim view of ELF skyjacking and instituted stringent security precautions. These produced shoot-outs in the air. At the same time through conventional diplomatic initiatives and less conventional secret coercion, Ethiopia sought to erode the support of the Eritrean rebels abroad, while internally pursuing an expanded hearts-and-minds anti-insurgency campaign—a multifaceted strategy that had not been without results until the army became distracted in 1974 by coup politics. The Israelis revealed even less restraint seeking out the fedayeen wherever they might be found, authorizing assassination, deep penetration raids into Arab states, air strikes on suspected headquarters, and a series of military operations that the neighboring Arab regimes chose not to interpret as acts of war. Coupled with the most stringent security precautions on El Al and in their diplomatic missions, the Israelis felt they could largely protect their own, erode fedayeen strength, and strike terror into terrorist hearts. In large part they were successful, forcing the fedayeen to move on to more vulnerable targets, victims who were innocent of their danger until too late. In Latin America, too, regimes have resorted to illicit and unsavory means to impose order—torture being a pronounced favorite. Denied in public, it is practiced in semiprivate not only to gain information or in the name of vengeance, but also to intimidate both those presently engaged in rebellion and their potential recruits. In both Brazil and Guatemala, officially tolerated vigilantes have been active, although in the latter case, despite 10,000 deaths, stability is by no means assured. Most responsible governments, however, have relied on conventional means. They have tightened security and hoped for the best.

Some have suggested that all terrorists, no matter what the risks or cost in lives—even innocent lives—be killed on sight. With *no* chance of escape, the attractions of spectacular, manipulative acts of terror might well decline except for the few suicidal revolutionary cadres. On the other hand, the certainty of punishment might attract the suicidal psychopath. More practical has been the Ethiopian policy of armed resistance and swift, cursory punishment, but even this has not proved foolproof. Others have applied the bilateral approach used by the United States in its cooperation with Cuba on air piracy. But even with such an agreement, full compliance cannot be assured. What would the reaction of America be to the commandeering of a Soviet jet filled with weeping, joyous Russian Jews pleading for passage to Israel? There are still those Americans who recall the screaming refugees from communism trucked back into Eastern Europe by bewildered American soldiers after World War II. And many countries are proud of long traditions of sheltering political refugees. Still, the Cuban-American experience demonstrates that concrete progress is possible through bilateral arrangements. There is less to be said for the impact of multilateral agreements or some of the other more daring innovations of the idealists of international law.

In the case of air piracy, for example, the 1963 Tokyo Convention on Offenses and Certain Acts Committed on Board Aircraft, which ostensibly required host countries to return hijacked planes and passengers, has had no visible effect. The 1970 Hague Draft Convention on Unlawful Seizure of Aircraft has not been ratified by a sufficient number of governments to be an effective deterrent. The 1971 Montreal Convention agreement that aviation sabotage be punished or the accused extradited has been equally ineffective. Two joint air-security conferences in Rome in 1973 produced meager results, even in light of what the State Department indicated were modest American expectations. As noted above, the United Nations has not developed a satisfactory definition of terrorism. It has not found a majority to support any form of resolution or even been able to demonstrate any great sense of urgency. Proposals for other international alternatives—a world criminal court, for example—however well intentioned or promising in theory, seem likely to be similarly ineffectual in the present climate. Still, many governments have not given up hope that at least a major part of the international community will in time take a firmer stand.

81

Because of the difficulties present in the big picture, the American focus has by necessity been on the minutiae of response—all the tiny incremental steps that go to protect the vulnerable. In the area of technology and methods, the result has been the proliferation of screening devices, airport guards, and passenger searches. Security has been paid for with discomfort and expense. Worldwide, such screening procedures vary immensely. Rome airport security had long been notoriously lax. On the other hand, passengers from London to Belfast must pass through perhaps the world's most intensive search, more rigorous even than the procedures of El Al. The Ethiopians also are strict, even on internal flights. The distressing fact is that one man who is willing to take disproportionate risks can slip through the system. There can never be absolute security, if only for the reason that as cost and inconvenience rise, diminishing returns set in, and "security" rather than terrorism would prevent the free flow of air traffic. This point has not yet been approached, however, nor have the limits of technology. New devices may be around the corner: computerized thumb-print identification may weed out the suspect with an altered passport or aircraft cabins may be equipped to fill with instantly incapacitating gas. Improved techniques alone can do a substantial job until revolutionary ingenuity devises a counter-technique or seeks new targets.

The growing use of the revolutionary tactic of kidnapping business executives has engendered a variety of counter-tactics. The American State Department has produced a five-page pamphlet, *General Security Tips for U.S. Businessmen Abroad*. For the most part, this pamphlet contains the conventional wisdom, but it is a beginning. There is also research under way, for example, on the kidnapper-hostage relationship, to locate areas where the common wisdom may be in error. In such studies, the policy of "women and children first" has come under question. The American government, on a variety of levels and by varying means, is pursuing an active interest in the problem of terrorism, seeking to discover appropriate tactics and perhaps even to fashion a coherent strategy.

The interest of the United States government in transnational terrorism developed with the rise in international air piracy and also as a result of such actions as the Lod and Munich massacres in 1972. The Nixon administration, elected on a law and order platform in 1968, saw such acts as unacceptable attacks against the fabric of international order. On 25 September 1972 the President set up the Cabinet Com-

82

Table 1

STATISTICAL SUMMARY OF CIVIL AIRCRAFT INCIDENTS

	1973 to Date	1972	1971	1970	1969	1968	1967	1961-66	1930-60
Hijackings									
U.S.	1	16	15	19	33	18	1	6	0
Foreign	14	18	10	40	42	12	5	9	45
Attempted hijackings									
U.S.	1	16	12	8	7	4	0	5	0
Foreign	6	14	22	19	9	1	1	9	5
Sabotage (includes attempts)									
U.S.	0	4	0	1	0	1	1	3	4
Foreign	0	7	6	10	3	2	3	5	18
Casualties [a]									
Passengers and crew									
Killed	101	140	8	88	2	2	66	191	217
Wounded	0	105	51	59	21	3	0	18	48
Hijackers and saboteurs									
Killed	4	17	7	5	5	0	0	1	5
Wounded	0	7	7	6	1	0	0	1	7
Origin of hijacked aircraft destined to Cuba									
U.S.	0	7	10	15	31	17	1	5	0
Other foreign	4	3	3	17	32	8	2	0	1

[a] Casualty figures include an estimate of casualties in connection with the hijacking of a Russian aircraft in May 1973.
Source: U.S. Department of State, 1 November 1973.

Table 2

BOARDING DENIALS, ARRESTS, AND SEIZURES RESULTING
FROM PASSENGER/BAGGAGE INSPECTION PROCEDURES

	Last Quarter 1972	First Quarter 1973
Passengers denied boarding	1,906	617
Passenger arrests	1,181	573
Weapons confiscated		
Guns	586	504
Knives	2,259	2,430
Explosives	5	30
Other	546	1,952
Total	3,396	4,916

Source: Office of the Secretary of Transportation, Director of Transportation Security, 6 June 1973.

mittee to Combat Terrorism, composed of the secretaries of state, treasury, defense, and transportation, the attorney general, the ambassador to the United Nations, the directors of the CIA and FBI, and the assistants to the President for national security affairs and domestic affairs. A subordinate Working Group on Terrorism, chaired by the representative of the State Department, was simultaneously established, giving the United States a focus for developing a counter-terrorism policy.

Beyond the working group, various military and civilian agencies, duly influenced by presidential concern, moved terror up on their priority lists, sought avowed experts, and assigned analysts to develop policy and coordinate intelligence. At the bidding of the commander in chief, the army accepted that combatting terror would be one of its missions during the next decade. The FBI, long interested in internal subversion, extended this interest to Irish-Americans involved in giving aid and comfort to the IRA. The Secret Service offered protective coverage to fifteen additional foreign dignitaries, created 115 additional fixed posts at Washington diplomatic missions, and at 23 additional UN missions in New York. Customs and postal employees were alerted to letter bombs, and the Department of Transportation required 100 percent screening of airline passengers and hand luggage. Visa regulations were tightened and further screening of foreigners seeking admission to the U.S. was introduced. For example, in January 1974 the president of Sinn Féin, the political wing of the Provisional Irish Republican Movement, had his visa revoked. Security at American missions and offices abroad was strengthened. The President submitted to Congress a request for $21 million to improve overseas security, as both officials and private citizens abroad were reminded of the possibility of terrorist action. Additional safeguards were also implemented at American military bases overseas, and a new program was initiated to place advanced controls on all tactical nuclear weapons to prevent their use by unauthorized personnel. There was, in fact, a rush towards whatever techniques and tactical steps could be implemented unilaterally.

Equally important was the coordinating of intelligence and the increased collection of intelligence specifically concerning potential terrorists. As part of this effort, secure teletypes between the Immigration and Naturalization Service and all involved agencies were installed. Cooperation in intelligence matters with such relevant international groups as INTERPOL, NATO, and the OAS and with individual governments was sought. Such liaison has had varying results, but those involved feel that a beginning has been made in tapping informers, who have always been the curse of revolutionary organizations.

In the area of contingency planning, the working group has sorted out federal jurisdiction so that the FBI is responsible for international terrorist acts in the United States and the administration of swift responses to requests for assistance in cases of emergency. There is an Emergency Watch Group to provide guidance, coordinate action, and communicate with foreign governments which may be involved. Contingency plans for responding to terrorist acts against American missions or installations abroad have also been devised.

At the moment, all contingency planning rests on the principle that the United States will not pay blackmail. When the three diplomats held in the Saudi embassy in Khartoum were murdered in 1973, the President announced, "This tragic event underscores once again the need for all nations to take a firm stand against the menace of international terrorism." [1] Elsewhere the most favored option has been to make innocent lives the first priority, even if instant and excessive concessions become necessary. So far Washington holds to the attitude that "the best diplomacy we can muster can save lives in both the short and the

---

[1] *New York Times*, 3 March 1973.

85

longer run." [2] Secretary of State Henry Kissinger in August 1975 even removed W. Beverly Carter, United States ambassador in Tanzania, who had dealt successfully through the parents of the hostages. He insisted that saving one life might later risk hundreds.

Another direction of American counter-terrorist diplomacy has been to try to bolster the ineffective multilateral agreements. This effort has been pursued in the UN, where the only resolution on the subject passed by the General Assembly provides for prosecution or extradition of those responsible for attacks and threats on diplomats. Known as the Convention on the Prevention and Punishment of Crimes against Internationally Protected Persons, including Diplomatic Agents, it is problematic whether it will prove any more effective than the various other conventions. Still, the United States considered this new treaty to be a real achievement.

Bilateral United States efforts to deny substantive concessions to manipulative terrorists have run into difficulties. For example, President Nixon, to no avail, urged Chancellor Bruno Kreisky of Austria to reconsider his decision to close the transit facilities for Soviet Jews, stating that "we simply cannot have governments—small or large—give in to international blackmail by terrorist groups." [3] Only the Israelis have held firmly to this hard line and, given the scope and intensity of their authorized counter-terror operations, today such company is not exactly an unmixed blessing in the international community.

The American mix of techniques and tactics essentially represents a collection of ad hoc responses. They do not comprise a coherent counter-strategy. The entire thrust is to combat the specific acts of men rather than the conditions which engender those acts. Thus the American response has not eroded the causes of revolutionary violence. Perhaps revolutionaries, like the demented and the criminal, will be with us always. There may be rebels without a cause who are beyond a remedial strategy, but there are far more rebels with a cause who are not. Consequently, the easing of rebel anguish and frustration—if possible—may in turn lessen rebel aggression.

Such a strategy will have a limited effect against terrorist acts, for example, perpetrated in the struggle for Palestine which has an inherent justice that can hardly be denied, even by most Israelis. If the Pales-

---

[2] Ambassador Lewis Hoffacker, speech, Regional Foreign Policy Conference, 27 October 1973, Madison, Wisconsin (mimeo.).
[3] *New York Times*, 3 October 1973.

tinians are repeatedly humiliated and regularly frustrated by their own incapacities and their opponents' arrogance, all the tactics devised by the guardians of order will not contain fedayeen terror. Thus the most effective anti-terrorist strategy available to America is a serious pursuit of some sort of Middle East solution that will guarantee the Arabs justice and the Israelis security—a grail which has been beyond anyone's grasp during the last generation. This is exactly the direction followed by Secretary Kissinger since October 1973. If an accommodation could be fashioned, the ground would begin to erode under terrorist feet. In the short run, this would be likely to cause a rise in terrorist operations; there would be an assault of desperate men determined to deny an unpalatable compromise. In the long run, there would hopefully be a decline in violence.

Unfortunately, it is quite beyond the bounds of possibility that the world could be so ordered as to satisfy *all* aspirations, slake every thirst, or assure every destiny. It is far easier to train the elite, supply the army, hope for the best, and be resigned to an imperfect order as preferable to none at all. Even if there is to be no new isolationism, Washington now appears to have other priorities, and correcting the world's injustices is low on the agenda.

Summary. There can be no easy policy recommendation that would guarantee American immunity from future terror. In general terms, the United States appears to face only a limited threat from domestic revolutionaries, although pathological politics and the violent deeds of the demented appear to be with us yet. While the future may see a return to the violent agitational politics of the last decade, in American politics riots, symbolic arson, and civil disobedience have never foreshadowed widespread resort to guns. It is more likely that revolutionaries from abroad, attracted by soft targets, may strike at what they see as the center of the imperialist-capitalist-racist conspiracy. Neither restrictive legislation nor domestic tranquility would then be of much use. The best protection, other than foreknowledge, would be more extensive and elaborate security. Few taxpayers, however, like to pay in advance of a problematical emergency, nor do many Americans like to restrict their personal liberties. Additional funding is desirable for federal law enforcement agencies, for research and development of technological aspects of defense, for intelligence on active and potential revolutionaries, and for research into the nature of revolutionary terrorism. And all efforts of the Working Group on Terrorism should be encouraged and where necessary expanded. If general international conventions prove ineffectual, as they have so far, then a more intensive program of bilateral agreements should be pursued. Yet there simply is no final solution to the sufficiently dedicated fanatic with a moment of luck.

There are, of course, a variety of remedies that will not work. However politically astute the introduction of the death penalty or harsh the new laws may be, a revolutionary is hardly going to be deterred, and the psychopath may actually be attracted. Nor is it necessarily likely that a firm no-bargaining policy will have the desired result. Would Washington refuse to bargain with a nuclear terrorist? Even the necessary and highly effective detection devices and visa techniques can do little more than screen out the incompetent and deter the timorous. As the Secret Service knows well, there is simply no absolutely certain way to protect potential targets, even by the most intensive security techniques. What is required is to devise a careful balance between reasonable protection and cost in funds and freedom—rather as the postal authorities have managed in Belfast where letterboxes, formerly sealed to prevent the placement of bombs, have been altered so that only thin letters can be mailed. Thus at a not unreasonable cost the mails slip through.

Any American response to terrorism must accept several ground rules. Because of third world perceptions of the international system, this country will remain a revolutionary target no matter what our posture; 1776 is very long ago, and even the Marshall Plan is ancient history to a young Palestinian Arab. Attacks on transnational order by rebels, often with built-in incapacities, must not be perceived as truly terminal threats to the system and can be tolerated like natural calamities. It is, of course, unwise to ignore natural calamities entirely, although it would be better to ignore such violence than overreact. Still, the American reaction, putting aside the public hysteria and the moral indignation of some in the government, has been largely reasoned, appropriate, and responsive to the present scope of the problem. Certain tactics may in time have to be adjusted or certain new measures employed, but also, over time, familiarity with the phenomenon will lead to a better perspective.

The more effectively stable the transnational system, the more desperate will be those with fading hopes for dreams denied and the more likely that they will strike out in sensational terrorist acts. Moreover, we live in times where technology has made possible both the magnification of violence and also created complex and vulnerable targets for that violence. It has become far more alluring for the frantic few to appear on the world stage of television than remain obscure guerrillas of the bush.

These new transnational terrorists may be countered with special techniques, technological innovation, the deployment of new knowledge, the enactment of new law, or by quiet diplomacy and discrete coercion, but hopefully not by recourse to counter-terror or means alien to traditional American sensibility. And perhaps where possible real efforts can be made to alleviate the legitimate grievances that fuel rebel frustrations. Most important, the threatened must accept that, however spectacular the deeds of terror, they are more easily tolerated than prevented.

Selected Readings

There is no single authoritative study of terror from any focus, although David C. Rapoport's *Assassination and Terrorism* (Toronto: Canadian Broadcasting Corporation, 1971) is an excellent introduction. A most interesting approach to the area is the staff report, *Assassination and Political Violence*, to the National Commission on the Causes and Prevention of Violence (New York: Bantam, 1970). Several of the works with appropriate titles (Roland Gaucher, *The Terrorists: From Tsarist Russia to the O.A.S.* [London: Secker and Warburg, 1968], and Edward Hyams, *Terrorists and Terrorism* [London: J. M. Dent, 1975]) are surveys, while more rigorous if tentative analytical attempts (Irving Louis Horowitz, "Political Terrorism and State Power," *Journal of Political and Military Sociology*, vol. 1 [Spring 1973], pp. 147–57) suffer from a lack of hard data. A most useful study is Carol Edler Baumann's *The Diplomatic Kidnappings: A Revolutionary Tactic of Urban Terrorism* (The Hague: Martinus Nijhoff, 1973). (See also: Peter Clyde, *An Anatomy of Skyjacking* [London: Abelard-Schuman, 1973]; and James A. Arey, *The Sky Pirates* [New York: Scribners, 1972].) Two works with a broader scope are most significant: Ted Robert Gurr, *Why Men Revolt* (Princeton: Princeton University Press, 1969) and E. V. Walter, *Terror and Resistance: A Study of Political Violence* (New York: Oxford University Press, 1969). And an excellent summary is *Civil Violence and the International System* (London: The International Institute for Strategic Studies, Adelphi Papers 82 and 83, 1971).